HIGHFIELD

NEW

INDUSTRIAL

AREA

ADEYFIELD

LEVERSTOCK GREEN

BENNETTS END

APSLEY

D

LONDON-BIRMINGHAM MOTOR ROAD

TO ST. ALBANS

TO LONDON

N
W E
S

Acknowledgements

The authors would like to acknowledge the help received from the following organisations in respect of the publication of "Hemel Hempstead: The Story of New Town Development 1947-1997":

> Dacorum Borough Council
> The Dacorum Heritage Trust
> Hemel Hempstead Local History and Museum Society
> Commission for the New Towns
> County Records Office, County Hall, Hertford
> Hertfordshire Library Service
> Hemel Hempstead Gazette

The following people have made a significant contribution towards the production of this book:

Mike Stanyon	Assistant Heritage Officer
	The Dacorum Heritage Trust
Matt Wheeler	Curator, The Dacorum Heritage Trust
David Wass	Town Centres Projects Manager
	Dacorum Borough Council
Colin Barnard	Director of Planning
	Dacorum Borough Council
Murray Litvak	Marketing Liaison Officer
	Commission for the New Towns
Pauline Sidell	Archivist, Dacorum Borough Council
James Doe	Senior Planning Assistant
	Dacorum Borough Council
Mike Browne &	Public Relations Dept.
Ben Garner	Dacorum Borough Council
Samantha McNeilly	County Record Office
Doris Mobbs	Leader of the 'Reminiscence Project'
Peter Drabble	Deputy Manager, Marlowes Centre

The photographer, David Spain, was commissioned to take some contemporary black and white photographs for this publication.

All the colour photography used in the book formed part of a separate commission undertaken by Kelly Cantlon.

The following individuals have also provided invaluable assistance by supplying us with photographs or information:

Bob Bennett, Rev. D. Bevington, Michael Blackman, Maggie Bull, Ron Griffiths, Geoff Lawrence, Pete Moules, Jasper Sawhney, Linda Sims, Peter Ward, Rev. J. Williams, Gwen Woods.

Foreword

This book is a window in time. Although the period from 1947 is very significant in the development of Hemel Hempstead, we should remember that the town has been a busy commercial centre for many hundreds of years. In my view, the designation of Hemel Hempstead as one of the first post-war New Towns compares in significance with the decision of Henry VIII, nearly 500 years ago, to grant the town a Charter.

The authors have done a superb job in delving into archives and turning mounds of dull and dusty agendas, minutes of meetings and reports into a very interesting and enjoyable account of the development of the New Town of Hemel Hempstead. I am sure you will find it fascinating.

Now that the New Town is here and celebrating its Fiftieth Anniversary, this is not the end of an era. The town today continues to evolve, driven forward by the initiative, energy and stamina of the people who live and work here. Perhaps fifty years from now there will be another book to be written. It will be about how the New Town matured and prospered. Perhaps you will be part of that story.

Cllr. Dick Dennison
The Worshipful Mayor of the Borough of Dacorum
July 1997.

Introduction

At the beginning of this year we were asked by the Dacorum Borough Council to produce a book which would document the story of New Town development in Hemel Hempstead. In accepting this commission we have aimed to provide the reader with a clear understanding of the process by which the small country town of Hemel Hempstead grew into the much larger and thriving modern community we know today. Beginning before the Second World War, the text aims to cover all the major themes and social implications involved as well as provide some insight into the development of each of the New Town neighbourhoods as they were built.

Our intention has been to produce a readable account which we hope will be of interest to local residents and their families as well as students and schoolchildren studying local history. We are fortunate to have been allowed to make use of the extensive photographic collections of the Dacorum Heritage Trust, the Hemel Hempstead Local History and Museum Society and Hemel Hempstead Library. This, together with access to the Commission for the New Towns' collection, held at the County Record Office, and the Borough Council's own archive, has enabled us to illustrate our text with a wide range of photographs. We are sure these will add to your enjoyment and understanding of the remarkable and unique story behind the creation of Hemel Hempstead New Town.

Scott Hastie & Lynne Fletcher
July 1997.

Contents

Historical Background

During the last few years some exciting archaeological finds have indicated an earlier pattern of settlement in the local area than was previously thought likely. In 1991, during construction of the A41 by-pass road, eight Neolithic sites were uncovered on the south-eastern slopes of the Gade and Bulbourne valleys. More recently the Herts Archaeological Trust, excavating in advance of building work above Gadebridge Park, uncovered a late Bronze Age site. This is now thought to have been an early farming settlement dating from 1200-700 BC, although the archaeological evidence is still being assessed. However a definite history of early settlement along the Gade valley, and in the Hemel Hempstead area in particular, has already been confirmed by significant Roman finds made at Boxmoor and Gadebridge.

The first discovery of local Roman habitation dates back to August 1837 when the remains of a Roman cremation were found. These were unearthed, by chance, in two coloured glass containers within the burial ground of Box Lane Chapel. This unusual find was added to in 1850, when the remains of a substantial Roman building and well were uncovered on ground which is now part of the forecourt at Hemel Hempstead Railway Station. One hundred years later in 1963, the site of a large Roman villa was found in Gadebridge Park during the construction of the second section of the Leighton Buzzard Road. The provision of this new link road, bypassing the brand new town centre in Marlowes, had led directly to the discovery of a significant Roman farming estate. It was a find of national archaeological importance.

The main building uncovered was a nine roomed villa which had been extensively modernised during the Fourth Century AD. This house had obviously been either a municipal facility or home to a very wealthy Roman, given that five of its rooms had the benefit of under floor heating systems. Excavations also revealed that from AD 325 it had been provided with its own large heated bathing pool. Roman pools of this type and size are very rare and, to date, it remains the only one of its kind to have survived in Britain. The only other comparable example is the famous municipal pool which is a major tourist attraction in the old Roman City of Bath. Building on the work of the earlier Nineteenth Century finds, the remains of two other First Century Roman buildings were uncovered in the grounds of Boxmoor House School and the forecourt of the railway station in 1966 and 1967 respectively.

Allied to their temperate climate and ready water supply, the fertile lands of the Gade and Bulbourne valleys were considered by the Romans to be an ideal location to establish several large farming estates. An additional advantage of the locality was its proximity to the major investment they had made at St. Albans, establishing the markets and facilities of the Roman City of Verulamium. The countryside around Hemel Hempstead became an important agricultural area where the Romans knew that their thorough organisation and methods could reap a rich and regular harvest. Despite this Roman influence, the name 'Hamelhamstede' is of later Saxon origin and means 'homestead of Hamel'. It is likely that any early settlement was part of the lands owned by Heamele, Bishop of Mercia, in the Eighth Century. We do know that the territory of Heamele was granted to the Bishop of London in AD 705 by Offa, King of Essex. At the time of the Norman Conquest, Haemele was held by two lieutenants of Earl Leofwin, the brother of King Harold. In the Domesday records of 1086, the community is listed as part of the much larger area of land which the Anglo Saxons had referred to as the 'Hundred of Dacorum'. It is from this historical reference that the District Council took its name, following its creation in the local government reorganisation of 1973.

Throughout the Norman and later Medieval periods, the small agricultural hamlet that grew up along the banks of the River Gade, between the two mills at the Bury and at Piccotts End, was part of the extensive agricultural lands that belonged to the monastery at Ashridge. Hemel Hempstead had no power base of its own and simply could not compete with the economic activity generated by the Royal patronage, which was already so strongly established in two neighbouring communities. To the north, at Berkhamsted, the Norman castle was a centre of great power and early prosperity, whilst to the south of Hemel Hempstead the Plantagenet Kings had erected a splendid palace and also founded a Royal hunting estate at Kings Langley. However this disadvantage to the town's development did not extend much beyond the beginning of the Fifteenth Century, as gradually the Royal residences in the Capital became more favoured by the Royal Court. As a consequence, by the time we reach the age of the great Tudor monarchs, both the neighbouring Royal establishments at Kings Langley and Berkhamsted had fallen into a state of disuse and dereliction.

It is thought that the patronage bestowed instead on Hemel Hempstead by King Henry VIII was inspired by a fondness for the area, it is alleged he developed when courting Ann Boleyn at Lockers. Certainly his award of Bailiwick status to the town in 1539 laid very important foundations. The key benefit of this Charter was that it allowed for a weekly market to be held in the town centre at Hemel Hempstead every Thursday. Following the Dissolution of the Monasteries which had closed down Ashridge and annexed its monastic estates, King Henry had become the new Lord of the Manor of Hemel Hempstead. He now had a direct financial incentive to help ensure the growing prosperity of the area and, with its thriving agricultural

Early drawing of Hemel Hempstead Market House.

market acting as a catalyst, the town soon went from strength to strength. In addition to a sheep and cattle fair on Holy Thursday, an annual pleasure fair was held on the feast day of Corpus Christi. Another later Charter, issued by Oliver Cromwell in 1656, granted Hemel Hempstead a further three fairs. Hemel Hempstead had now become firmly established as the principal trading centre for the area, where all the local farmers would come to do business, tipping their corn and barley into what is now the cellars of the old Town Hall. A written account, provided by an unknown traveller in 1742, describes the town as having "the greatest corn market in the County, or perhaps in England". In 1822 William Cobbett referred to the local soil as "the very best corn land we have in England".

The foundation stone for the Town Hall was laid in 1851 on the site of the old Corn Exchange building in the High Street and the Jacobean style structure was constructed in stages, as funds became available, during the period 1851-88. Hemel Hempstead's Bailiwick status survived until 13th July 1898 when it was superseded by a Charter granted by Queen Victoria which established a Mayor and Corporation. From this date the Borough of Hemel Hempstead was created with its own Mayor and Bailiff, Aldermen and Burgesses. The stone fountain which stood in the Broadway, close to the southern entrance to Gadebridge Park, was presented to the town in 1898. Two local residents, Ann and Helen Varney, paid for this monument to help commemorate the creation of Hemel Hempstead as a borough. Hemel Hempstead's borough status was lost in 1973 when, following local government reorganisation, Dacorum District Council was formed. However the town's proud heritage was regained eleven years later when Dacorum was granted borough status. The first Mayor of the Borough of Dacorum, Charles Barling, was appointed in October 1984 and the new local authority was then able to properly inherit the ancient charters and regalia that had been maintained in the interim by the Charter Trustees. The old town hall had remained the hub of local administrative affairs until the New Town planners' long promised Civic Centre development finally opened in Marlowes in 1966. The old Town Hall subsequently became the Hemel Hempstead Arts Centre which opened in September 1978.

The most historic building which survives intact in Hemel Hempstead is the Parish Church of St. Mary which is situated just behind the High Street. This is a splendid example of Norman church architecture, dating from 1140 to 1180, and is certainly one of the oldest and finest churches in Hertfordshire. The aisled nave has remained almost entirely as the original and the base of the central tower also still dates from the Twelfth Century. The top of the 70ft. church tower was once embattled in the Fourteenth Century when a magnificent timber framed spire was added. This spire, which was releaded in 1985, rises a further 130ft. above the parapet and is a beautiful example of an early fluted timber spire covered in lead.

The story of the town's other principal historic building dates back to the Sixteenth Century. Henry VIII's own gentleman priest, the Rector of Ashridge Thomas Waterhouse, lived at the Bury with his family following the dissolution of the monastery. In 1540 Thomas' brother-in-law, Richard Combe, bought the Bury from the Crown, together with its land and gardens, brew-house, bake-house and mill for the princely sum of £108. A fourteen room Elizabethan mansion was subsequently built on the site by Sir Richard Combe in 1595. The Sixteenth Century gatehouse near the entrance to Gadebridge Park, together with some contemporary walling from the old Manor House which enclose ornamental gardens, is all that remains of this old Bury structure which was pulled down in 1791 by William Ginger. The replacement he built, also called the Bury, survives to this day and is situated on Queensway, just off the link road between the Leighton Buzzard Road and Marlowes. It currently serves as the District's Registry Office.

Despite the strong historic traditions maintained by Hemel Hempstead as a prosperous town in Hertfordshire, there was still a real danger that the proposed post war arrival of such a massive New Town development could damage and distort the community's sense of the past. To their credit the

St Mary's Church, Hemel Hempstead.

The Bury Ruins, Hemel Hempstead.

local authorities and the New Town planners were always sensitive to this issue and, as proof of this, the architectural integrity of the High Street still survives today as one of the most unspoilt and attractive historic streets in Hertfordshire. As a direct consequence of a disastrous fire which occurred in 1749, most of the buildings in the High Street date from the mid Eighteenth and Nineteenth Centuries. However, it would still be true to say that some elements of older structures survive behind these later frontages. The fabric and appearance of many of these properties were thoroughly renovated in a major overhaul of the High Street which was organised and financed jointly by the Commission for the New Towns, Civic Trust and the local authorities in 1968.

An interesting example of long standing conservation in the High Street is an old water pump; one of two made by local ironfounder Joseph Cranstone. This communal pump, at the northern higher end of the High Street, was fed from a deep well and supplied drinking water, which was unavailable from the surface wells within most High Street properties. Prior to the Nineteenth century, these smaller domestic wells became all too easily contaminated with undrained sewage running down the hill. The well stand was later used as a base for a working lamp, when gas lighting was first introduced to the High Street in 1835. It still stands at the far end of the lower sunken side of the main street, which itself presents an unusual and attractive aspect, adding to the architectural charm of the area. The future for these and many other interesting features should now be secure, given that the entire High Street area is now officially designated as one of Dacorum's twenty-three Conservation Areas.

Sitting just below the High Street lies Gadebridge Park, three hundred acres of which was purchased by the Borough Council from the Paston Cooper estate in 1952. This was another key historic asset which the New Town planners were careful to safeguard for the future inhabitants of Hemel Hempstead. Today's public parklands were formerly part of the estate of Gadebridge, which had been purchased in 1811 by the leading surgeon of the day, Astley Paston Cooper. As a doctor who regularly attended Royalty, as well as the aristocracy of the nation, Paston Cooper was an immensely wealthy and influential local personality. He was made a Baronet in 1821, having conducted a successful operation to remove a tumour from the head of King George IV. Sir Astley died on 12th February 1841 at the age of 73. Following his funeral at Guys Hospital, the family hatchment was fixed to the north wall of the south transept in St. Mary's Church. A statue to his memory was placed in St. Paul's Cathedral and a further monument installed at St. Mary's Parish Church. Sir Astley, who produced no heir, had nominated his nephew Astley to inherit the bulk of his fortune and his Baronetcy. A later great nephew, also Astley Paston Cooper, became the first

Mayor of the town in 1898. During his tenure as Mayor, this third generation Paston Cooper owned over 1000 acres of land in Hemel Hempstead.

In 1809, when John Dickinson purchased Apsley Mill, he founded a paper making industry which was to become the dominant local employer for over 150 years. The stationery manufacturing business which developed from this first base in Apsley went on to become a world leader, enjoying vast international markets. The coming of the canal in 1797 and the arrival of the railway in 1837, were other key local developments within a nation-wide process of Industrial Revolution which helped to stimulate a major shift in economic emphasis for the town of Hemel Hempstead. Local farmers and major land owners like Sir Astley Paston Cooper at Gadebridge had been vehement in their opposition to the noisy railways in particular. Paston Cooper simply refused to countenance the intrusion of such "infernal machinery" across the tranquil pastures of his estates. He also had the social connections to ensure that the original plans for routing the London to Birmingham railway along the Gade valley were firmly blocked in the House of Lords. Such staunch resistance ensured that this artery of communication was kept well away from the town centre. However the construction of two such major transport links meant that Hemel Hempstead's commercial expansion westwards to meet them, together with the development of both Boxmoor and the industrial suburb of Apsley, was inevitable. It is safe to say that the growth of the town along Marlowes is a process that would have evolved with, or without, the stimulation of New Town development during the second half of the Twentieth Century.

THE BOROUGH OF HEMEL HEMPSTEAD

Hemel Hempstead High Street and Town Hall, circa 1905.

Hemel Hempstead High Street and Market, circa 1905.

Hemel Hempstead High Street, looking south, 1968.

John Hooper, last Mayor and Bailiff of Hemel Hempstead and Charles Kirk, retiring Town Clerk, on the last day that Hemel Hempstead was a Borough, 31st March 1976.

Ideas and Opposition

The best of the elements which are woven into the theory of New Town planning owe a considerable debt to several major philanthropic industrialists of the Eighteenth and Nineteenth Centuries, who provided model communities for their employees. The most well-known examples of this practice in England are Bourneville, near Birmingham founded in 1897 by the confectioner George Cadbury and Port Sunlight built circa 1888 by Lord Leverhulme for the employees of his soap manufacturing company. Locally Lady Marion Alford of the Ashridge estate followed very similar principles, when she financed and personally designed the renovations of many tenant's properties in the garden village of Little Gaddesden. She herself was inspired by several examples of model villages she had seen on her travels in Switzerland. The Rothschild family had a similar benevolent influence on the local communities of Tring and Wigginton. The man credited as the modern originator of the New Town movement itself was Ebenezer Howard. In 1898 he wrote his seminal work "Tomorrow: A Peaceful Path to Real Reform" which was later retitled "Garden Cities of Tomorrow". In 1889 he had already helped to form the Garden City Association which was to pave the way for the first Garden City at Letchworth in 1903/4. His ideas proved very successful and the establishment of Welwyn Garden City soon followed in 1919/20.

New Town development was very relevant to the work of Lord Reith, the Minister for Works and Buildings, who in 1940 was charged with the responsibility of reporting to the Government on viable and preferred methods of post war reconstruction. Partly as a result of Lord Reith's preliminary recommendations, the Ministry of Town and Country Planning was created by the Government in 1943. It was the responsibility of his department to oversee national policy in this area, aided by new powers gained in the Town and Country Planning Act 1944. By this time the London County Council had also commissioned reports and investigations on the future of the Capital. In 1944 they published the Greater London Plan which was written by Professor Patrick Abercrombie. The principal recommendation of his report was to move a total of one million people out of London and re-settle them in a circle of eight new satellite towns, which it proposed should be built around the Capital. The structure of the plan was based on the principle of four concentric rings: an inner ring comprising the L.C.C. area and a suburban ring stretching out about twelve miles from Charing Cross. The third ring consisted chiefly of Green Belt land and it was followed by a final outer country ring which included the Hemel Hempstead area.

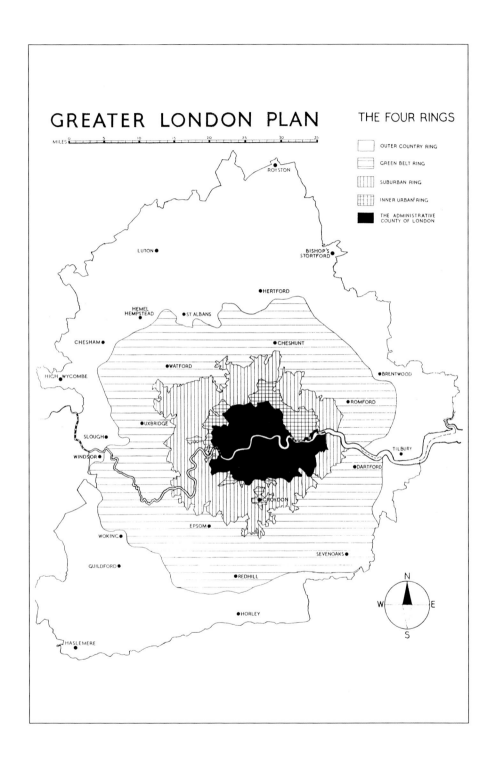

GREATER LONDON PLAN

MILES

THE FOUR RINGS

OUTER COUNTRY RING

GREEN BELT RING

SUBURBAN RING

INNER URBAN RING

THE ADMINISTRATIVE
COUNTY OF LONDON

ROYSTON

LUTON

BISHOP'S
STORTFORD

HERTFORD

HEMEL
HEMPSTEAD   ST ALBANS

CHESHAM

CHESHUNT

WATFORD

HIGH WYCOMBE

BRENTWOOD

ROMFORD

UXBRIDGE

SLOUGH

TILBURY

WINDSOR

DARTFORD

CROYDON

EPSOM

WOKING

SEVENOAKS

GUILDFORD

REDHILL

HORLEY

HASLEMERE

N
W   E
S

Closer to home, and as early as 1938, the local Borough Council had begun drawing up plans of their own to attract new industry and expand the housing capacity of Hemel Hempstead from 20,000 to 50,000. The local politicians had also not been slow to spot the potential hazards of London's social problems being allowed to encroach upon the character and composition of their own town. Back in 1922 at his Annual Banquet held in the Town Hall, the Mayor and Bailiff of Hemel Hempstead, had made the following heart-felt statement: "I pledge that the town of Hemel Hempstead will not become a receptacle for London's surplus". It is then perhaps ironic that, immediately after the Second World War, there seemed little threat of this happening. Abercrombie's report to the London County Council was rather scathing in its assessment of the potential of Hemel Hempstead in particular. He considered the locality to be "a scattered working class community, characterised by cheap ribbon development, which showed no regard for the siting of houses in relation to the contours". Furthermore it was his view that it was not a town to be developed, given the narrowness of the local valleys and the problematic hilly nature of the area. The existing industrial zones in the district were assessed as relatively inaccessible and the report described much of the Gade valley area as being "derelict". It was Abercrombie's opinion that Watford was a much more viable location around which to build an expanded industrial base.

The Professor's initial assessment had therefore pointed to the need to identify an alternative residential location for the proposed New Town. The communities of Tring, Wigginton and Aldbury were all given careful consideration because of their excellent transport links, served as they still are by the former main A41 road, railway and canal. However it is heartening to know that, some fifty years ago, conservation issues triumphed. The destruction of prime agricultural land and extensive areas of scenic beauty was considered significant enough to discount these locations. Eventually Abercrombie settled on promoting Redbourn in his plan as the only suitable site in the countryside to the north-west of London. Unfortunately this idea found no favour locally and soon ran into stiff resistance. The Town Planning Committee of Hertfordshire County Council reported that the people of West Hertfordshire "were not much in favour of a New Town at Redbourn". In addition to this the Redbourn site was considered too small and 37% of the proposed area already fell within the Borough of Hemel Hempstead. By 1945 the Hertfordshire County Council and the Mid Herts Joint Planning Committee had both declared their official opposition to the creating of a New Town at Redbourn. These two organisations instead favoured a carefully planned expansion of existing communities which they felt could still cope with the expected addition of up to 60,000 people, together with the associated employment and industrial infrastructure.

In April 1945 Alderman Fletcher echoed the fears of many residents regarding the potential loss of "the rural nature of the neighbourhood" and voiced his concern that "the proposed New Town could become a second Dagenham!". The local committee established by Hemel Hempstead Borough Council presented its own report in July 1945. This suggested that Hemel Hempstead should instead aim to expand its potential by seeking to gradually extend its boundaries to include Bovingdon, Flaunden, Leverstock Green, Water End and Great Gaddesden. At a national level, planning was still proceeding in earnest. The new Labour Government, elected in 1945, had now appointed a New Town Committee under the Chairmanship of Lord Reith. The brief of this Committee was to work with a real sense of urgency and it responded by producing a series of three separate reports within a ten month period. All this rapid ground work made it possible for the Government to pass the New Towns Act in 1946. This was the key legislation which sanctioned the establishment of a separate Development Corporation for each proposed New Town.

The Act also gave the new Corporations licence to acquire sites large enough for complete towns, together with the development power to create new housing, commercial and industrial areas from scratch. The Corporations were also given unique powers to acquire land at existing use value, rather

Lord Reith, 1951.

19

THIS IS URGENT !

CITIZENS OF HEMEL HEMPSTEAD

WHAT DOES THE "NEW TOWN" MEAN

TO YOU

?

Were You Consulted ?

Do You Want It ?

Do You Win—or Lose ?

TURN OVER AND READ THE
FACTS

Issued by The Hemel Hempstead Protection Association, Hon. Sec., K. Wyndham-Kaye, 74, Alexandra Road, Hemel Hempstead, and Printed by Hertfordshire Newspapers, Ltd., 39, Marlowes, Hemel Hempstead.

than market value, which was a considerable advantage. It was the New Town Committee's specific recommendation that these Corporations should become the owners of the site of each town and control their development, via their considerable powers as landlord. However it is important to realise that these new Corporations were not intended to replace the local authorities who would continue to be elected within the towns and districts relevant to each new community. The intention was to create a spirit of partnership, within the democratic process, which would help build a new consensus around planning for the future.

On 27th July 1946 a meeting took place between Mr. Lewis Silkin, the Minister of Town and Country Planning, and local Borough Councillors at Hemel Hempstead. This initial dialogue paved the way for the publication of a draft Designation Order on 27th September 1946. Issued under the auspices of the New Towns Act 1946, it designated a total of 7930 acres, including Hemel Hempstead, to be allocated for the construction of a New Town. The acquisition of this land was planned to allow for an expansion of the existing population of 20,000 to a total of 60,000 over an approximate ten year period. The work of the new Development Corporations was to be financed by specially sanctioned Treasury loans which were repayable over sixty years.

Following the publication of the Draft Order, a round of public consultation took place. These aimed to gather up all the more informal opinions of the various local government bodies, offices and members. They also provided every individual in the community with an opportunity to air his or her views on the matter. A major public meeting was held on 19th November at Dickinson's Apsley Guild House; this being the only local building large enough to accommodate the numbers expected. A large and vociferous crowd of approximately 1500 local people turned up to hear the Minister, Mr. Lewis Silkin, outline the background history and rationale for the current New Town proposal. A considerable amount of time was spent justifying the abandonment of the Redbourn option. It was explained that because Redbourn was already located between the three other significant communities of St. Albans, Harpenden and Hemel Hempstead, there was a real risk that its expansion could turn the entire area into one huge urban conglomerate. Sir Patrick Abercrombie was also quoted at the meeting, despite his early scepticism, as now agreeing with the latest proposal to site the New Town at Hemel Hempstead.

Many in the audience at the Guild Hall remained unconvinced. A common concern was "just how many undesirables" there were to be among the influx of 30,000 Londoners? The most widespread fear was the amount of demolition of older properties that would inevitably be required; the older people in particular feared change. Some of this concern was later justified.

There is an often remembered tale of one poor old lady who had to be physically removed from her house in Alma Road to make way for redevelopment in Marlowes. One resident who was present at the meeting remembers: "I was there with over 1000 people at Dickinson's Apsley Guild House. We felt like we needed a New Town like we needed a hole in the head!" Local farmers were also very concerned and puzzled by the suggested loss of more than 5000 acres of agricultural land, particularly at a time of national food shortages. Another early irritant was that: "local people were not eligible and that the modern houses to be built for the new residents were a source of envy from some of those still living in older houses without mod cons". There was also a general anxiety that the sheer number of people arriving from London would dominate the political scene and simply take over the town. Some of this friction did materialise and, as one elderly gentleman remembers: "when the people first moved in from London they said we resented them and used to call us 'Swede Bashers'!". However another local resident recalls: "I felt sorry for all the poor folk in London who had lost so much in the War and realised that they had to have somewhere to live...."

To address these and many other concerns, a Public Inquiry was set up on 2nd December 1946. Despite the fact that the Hemel Hempstead Gazette's editorial of that week declared confidently that "everyone had received a fair hearing", the Inquiry only lasted a total of three days! The Inspector's decision was issued at an informal press conference, held at the Ministry of Town and Country Planning on Thursday 4th February 1947. The following day the Draft Order authorising the use of the land around Hemel Hempstead was confirmed. The total acreage initially required had been reduced to 5910, but the New Town was to go ahead more or less as originally planned. At this time the rateable value of the Borough was given as £134,000 with a total population of 21,000.

At the beginning of March 1947 an announcement was made declaring that the Hemel Hempstead Protection Association was to appeal against the findings of the Public Inquiry. On 17th March 1947 an application was made to the High Court on the grounds that there had been insufficient consultation with the local authorities, as required by the New Towns Act. The Appeal was held on 14th, 15th and 16th July, before being dismissed on the 30th July 1947. The Attorney General, Sir Hartley Shawcross, appearing for the Government, solemnly declared that "these designation orders must unhappily mean hardship for the few". Rather starkly he is also recorded as saying in his judgement: "It may well mean that the village of Hemel Hempstead must die in order that Greater London may live"....

View of Marlowes prior to New Town development.

Shops at the bottom of Marlowes, showing Nicky Line viaduct (right).

Aerial view of the old town of Hemel Hempstead.

No time was lost making a start on the project once this important legal barrier had been removed. The day after the Attorney General's judgement Mr. W. O. Hart, General Manager of the Development Corporation, announced plans to establish a labour camp for the construction workers who would be needed for the first phase of the building work. The Development Corporation had already been formally established on 6th March 1946, under the Chairmanship of Lord Reith, so it was in a position to act immediately. Despite the initial impetus for the project provided by its success in the High Court, the early days of the Corporation were fraught with difficulties. These featured further legal delays relating to the detail of New Town planning at Hemel Hempstead and were compounded by a national economic crisis, which led to an acute shortage of labour, materials and central Government funding.

Although there was still widespread concern amongst the existing residents of the area, it is fair to say that at a local political level there was some solid and progressive support for the New Town initiative. As already discussed, local Councillors before the war were keenly aware of the need to expand the town and develop more employment in order to help build local prosperity. In embracing the New Town proposal they would be able to plan on a more ambitious level than they could ever have managed independently. They also knew that by following this path they could gain access to significant levels of central Government funding which would have otherwise been unobtainable. In this respect we can see that the majority of the local Councillors of the day acted with considerable foresight. According to the Hemel Hempstead Gazette of the time, this was in direct contrast to developments occurring in the east of the County, at Stevenage, where local Councillors were said to be fighting a much fiercer and more negative campaign to avoid becoming a New Town. The more positive attitude at Hemel Hempstead was best epitomised by Town Clerk, Mr. Charles Kirk, when he addressed the newly reformed Chamber of Commerce in 1946. He told them that he felt confident that "the New Town proposals would bring substantial benefit to the Borough and all its shopkeepers". Charles Kirk is an outstanding figure in the recent history of Hemel Hempstead. When appointed in 1939 he was the youngest Town Clerk in the Country, holding this office for 35 years. At his memorial service in 1986 former Mayor Gilbert Hitchcock CBE was inspired to say "The success of Hemel Hempstead owes much to the drive and ability of Charles Kirk".

The General Planning Consultant for the Hemel Hempstead New Town was the architect and landscape designer, Mr. G. A. Jellicoe, who was appointed by the Ministry of Town and Country Planning on 4th October 1946. He produced his Master Plan and accompanying report, based around the neighbourhood principle, in June 1947. These first documents also included a major landscape study by Miss Sylvia Crowe. As part of further public consultation exercises, details of the plans were exhibited at the Town Hall between 30th September and 14th October 1947. Local residents were invited to inspect the plans and offer their opinions. At the Mayor's Banquet, held in November 1947, Lord Reith confirmed that the Master Plan was not yet settled and would be modified in the light of comments received. At the end of November Sir Stafford Cripps, the Chancellor of the Exchequer, decreed that only essential preliminary work for the New Towns, such as sewage schemes and water mains could be carried out because of the national financial crisis. The first contracts for the construction of a workers' hostel, together with some initial roads and sewers at Hemel Hempstead then had a total value of £86,000. Funding difficulties had already delayed the Corporation's plans to acquire temporary housing to help accommodate the construction workforce.

Despite the inability to build in 1948, advance planning was still continuing for three new neighbourhoods at Adeyfield, Bennetts End and Chaulden. Detailed plans were also emerging for parts of the new town centre which were to be built along Marlowes. These outline plans were submitted to the Minister in August 1949 and modified at his request. A further round of public consultations was being undertaken with neighbouring authorities to discuss these detailed proposals and another Public Inquiry opened on 15th November 1949. The Borough Council, the local Chamber of Commerce, the Hemel Hempstead Protection Society and various other organisations all disputed aspects of the Master Plan. In particular, there were strong reservations about the siting of the proposed new railway station at Two Waters, whilst the amount of demolition required in the new shopping area also caused much controversy. However at the conclusion of the Inquiry, the Inspector found in favour of the Development Corporation and the project was able to move forward again.

Modifications to the Outline Plan of 1949 were published in September 1951. These plans now included more detailed proposals for the development of neighbourhoods at Adeyfield, Bennetts End, Chaulden, Counters End and some of Gadebridge. The plan also contained some revised and less ambitious ideas for the rebuilding of Marlowes. When building work began in 1949, there were still mixed feeling among the local residents. A typical comment was: "Once construction work on the New Town finally started, it was obvious that the quiet lifestyle of Hemel Hempstead would be changed forever". Another resident remembers that "We were sorry to see the countryside disappearing, but realised that people had got to live somewhere".

Whilst the 1947 Master Plan created the basic structure of the New Town and outlined the principles to be used in its construction, the revised plans of 1951, which were finally approved in June 1952, became the key document. They defined in detail the new and evolving shape of Hemel Hempstead throughout the next decade. These plans are not to be confused with a second Master Plan, which was issued ten years later. This additional plan was submitted to the Minister on 12th August 1960, when the first phase of the New Town development had been completed and the population of Hemel Hempstead had reached 60,000. The purpose of the later plan was to make provision for a further growth in population levels which had not been forecast or built into the earlier plans. The eventual population figure of Hemel Hempstead was now predicted to reach 80,000 by the early 1980's. Responsibility for organising this additional expansion fell to the Commission for the New Towns, which took over from the Hemel Hempstead Development Corporation in April 1962. At this point the Hertfordshire County Council also became more involved in the future planning of the town.

Back in 1947 Lord Reith had managed to find a motto for the new Development Corporation. After seeking out various suggestions, he settled upon "Majora, Uberiora, Pulchriora", which has been translated as "Greater, Richer, More Beautiful". It was in this spirit that, in 1949, the New Town planners set about building a New Town community on the empty fields around Hemel Hempstead.

Arms of Hemel Hempstead Development Corporation.

The Master Plan

Geoffrey Jellicoe's Master Plan of 1947 is careful to make a detailed assessment of the surrounding landscape and natural environment for the proposed New Town. It identifies a rolling plateau of agricultural land, intersected by steep chalk valleys. It noted that the bulk of well grown local timber could be found on the richer lands of the higher levels, given that the valley sides were covered by a thinner layer of poorer soil. Close attention was to be paid to landscaping, both in the preparation of schemes surrounding new development sites, and in the careful preservation of existing trees. Although there was no sizeable woodland in Hemel Hempstead, the area was described as well timbered with plenty of examples of well grown oak, ash and holly trees. In those days, prior to the outbreak of Dutch Elm Disease in the late 1960's, fine elm trees were common. These grew mainly in the rich soils of the higher terrain. Chestnuts were plentiful in the valleys and beech trees could be found scattered throughout the whole area. It was planned to plant many thousands of new young trees, hedge plants and shrubs, as well as over 200 acres of grass as the New Town progressed. The natural geography of the local area was an essential element woven into the Master Plan. Screens of trees and areas of open space, together with the steep slopes of the local hills surrounding the old town, were all to be incorporated in the overall design. These natural features were used by the planners to help make each of the proposed new neighbourhood areas distinct from one another, and from the town centre itself.

The task that faced the planners at Hemel Hempstead differed from that of most of the other Development Corporations, in that a considerable proportion of the designated area (approximately one third) was already built on and developed. Unlike the majority of Britain's other New Towns, Hemel Hempstead was already a thriving community of 20,000 people with a proud history and a prosperous market centre. Clearly then, Geoffrey Jellicoe did not have the advantage of beginning with an empty green field site in this case. He needed to take care to respect the community's heritage and traditions, as he laid down his plans to expand the town's population to 60,000 over a ten to fifteen year period. As a consequence the Master Plan showed the old town shopping centre preserved around the High Street, with the retention of the Town Hall building and St. Mary's Church. The plan did however prescribe some redevelopment to the east side of the High Street, in the form of some small squares and terraces.

In contrast Marlowes, which was then a rather run-down subsidiary trading area, including some low grade domestic buildings, was to be completely redesigned as a modern shopping boulevard. Today it may come as a surprise to realise that Princes Street in Edinburgh was quoted as the

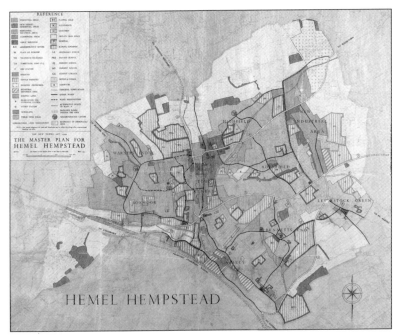

The Master Plan of 1947.

inspiration behind the initial plans for the new centre of Hemel Hempstead New Town! To be fair, Jellicoe's vision of a more grandiose and elegant town centre was vetoed by the Government as being impractical and too expensive. An ambitious array of civic buildings was originally planned, together with artificial lakes and ornamental water gardens, all of which would be designed to run along the west side of Marlowes. These included a new Civic Centre and Assembly Hall, two theatres, an art gallery and a library. All the shops were originally to be located on the east side of Marlowes, together with adjacent blocks of flats. Rather futuristically, there was also provision for two helicopter pads, one at each end of the town centre.

The Master Plan revealed Jellicoe's intention to expand the population by creating six new residential areas or 'neighbourhoods' around the town centre. Each of these had been planned to house a population of between five and ten thousand people. The largest of the proposed neighbourhoods lay to the east of the town at Adeyfield. To the north-east, Highfield was identified and to the south-east, Bennetts End, Warners End and Chaulden were in the western sector of the New Town, whilst Gadebridge lay to the north-west. These six new neighbourhoods were to join the existing residential suburbs at Apsley, Boxmoor and Leverstock Green. Each of these three areas would also be expected to contribute to the increased housing need with additional

Map of Great Britain showing New Town locations.

development plans which were designed to meet their own individual characteristics. For example, it was made clear that Leverstock Green should retain its pleasant village character. The village green was to be protected and a selection of larger houses specified, in order to help attract and retain middle income groups. It was a declared intention to provide each of the new neighbourhoods with its own shopping centre and public buildings, as well as open space for public gardens, recreation and allotments.

The New Town at Hemel Hempstead was deliberately designed to avoid monotony. Each of the new neighbourhoods was to have its own layout which would not be repeated elsewhere. The regular alignment of houses grouped in differing combinations along a sweeping road, a close or a cul-de-sac were all employed to help give variety to the new residential areas. In addition to this, efforts were made to vary the design of the new houses and flats, with a variety of different construction materials being used wherever possible. The range of new dwellings to be provided extended from small bedsitter flats built in three storeys, through to large three and four bedroomed houses with garages. However the majority of properties consisted of two and three bedroomed houses of around 750 sq.ft. in dimension. Most of these were built in short terraces, with some garages provided in groups. The accommodation was to be roughly in the proportion of 33% two bedroomed, 47% three bedroomed and 10% four bedroomed houses; with 10% of the total capacity being reserved for flats and old people's bungalows. There were some large semi-detached houses of 1000 sq.ft. together with a small amount of larger detached houses for sale, with garages included. Approximately half of the new housing was to be for sale, the other half being available for rental from the Commission for the New Towns. The initial building programme covered five years, but the Master Plan included an outline programme for the next fifteen years. Housing density to be achieved was specified at twelve dwellings per acre at Adeyfield, rising to 15 houses per acre subsequently. A target population was included for each neighbourhood: Adeyfield was to be the largest with an planned population of 10,000 people, Warners End: 6,250, Gadebridge: 5,900, Bennetts End: 5,300, Highfield: 5,200 and Chaulden: 4,950 residents.

Each of the neighbourhoods was to have its own infant and junior schools and there were to be new secondary schools built at Highfield, Adeyfield and Boxmoor. At this stage the main education campus for the New Town was to be at Bennetts End, where it was planned to build a total of four schools. The Master Plan also indicated that, in principle, there should be one Church of England church per 8-10,000 population. It was also made clear that a Roman Catholic church should be provided in the central area and one or more non-conformist chapels be established per neighbourhood. However none of the sites for these proposed religious buildings were specified within the detail of the Plan and their locations were left to evolve naturally as the neighbourhoods progressed.

In addition to the open space allocated in each neighbourhood, the 1947 Plan also made recommendations with regard to developing major recreational facilities within the New Town. The open land at Gadebridge was identified as central to the objective, whilst the proposed artificial lake and water gardens would provide additional recreational features close to the town centre. The Plan suggested that the moorland at Boxmoor should be cleared of restrictions, in order to become a summer resort area with boating and bathing facilities. It identified land in the central landscape reserve, close to the new industrial area, which it advised could be used for a possible sports stadium and associated developments. The Plan also noted that the two fine parklands, belonging to the independent fee-paying schools at Westbrook Hay and Abbots Hill, were some of the most desirable green spaces in the area. It recommended that they should be brought into public ownership as soon as possible.

The 1947 Master Plan carried proposals on how local transport should be upgraded to help serve an expanding Hemel Hempstead more efficiently. Two circular roads were planned to run around the New Town. An inner ring road was designed to enable travel between each residential neighbourhood; this would also link together the majority of places of public assembly outside the central area. An outer perimeter road was also considered essential. This would run around the fringe of the new urban areas, serving both as a by-pass and as an ideal route for industrial traffic. The establishment of these two ring roads was a key strategic issue for the planners and the report stated quite firmly that "in principle existing local roads should have continuity within residential areas only. All local road connections across this inner circular road should be broken". New main roads into town were to be deliberately punctuated by open land. This created green entry points to Hemel Hempstead, which it was hoped would emphasise the garden city aspect of the New Town.

Jellicoe considered that the four principal existing roads serving the town were all unsatisfactory. These were the A41 to London, the A414 to St. Albans, the B486 to London and the B487 to Redbourn. He expected that in the future the main approach to Hemel Hempstead, both from London and the North, would be via the new London to Birmingham motorway, planning for which was already well advanced. The motorway link from London would replace the existing St. Albans Road, whilst the link from the North would relieve traffic from the Redbourn Road. The Plan also suggested that the A41 should be diverted south of the railway and that the existing road through Apsley be redesignated to become a no-through road, serving the industrial estate only.

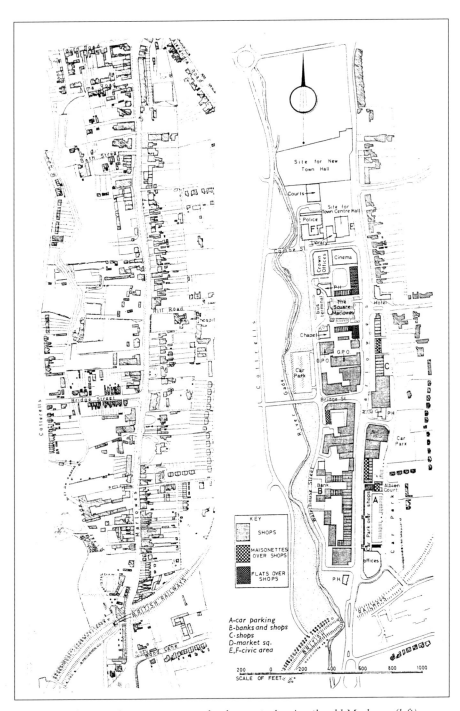

Plan of proposed new town centre development, showing the old Marlowes (left).

Given the relatively recent completion of the A41 by-pass in 1993, it is interesting to realise that this new road, pencilled in to the south of the railway, was to become part of the Ministry of Transport's proposed new radial road. This means that over fifty years ago, there were serious plans to connect Aylesbury to London, by-passing the communities of Tring, Berkhamsted, Hemel Hempstead and Kings Langley.

Jellicoe's ideas for changes to the local railway services caused considerable controversy. He wanted to demolish the existing LMS station at Boxmoor and replace it with a new central passenger station at Two Waters. This new station would also service the old Midland Line trains which linked Hemel Hempstead to Harpenden. Given that these old 'Nicky Line' trains no longer carried passengers, it was proposed that its services should in future terminate at the new industrial area to the east of the town. It was acknowledged that the logical location of a goods station serving Hemel Hempstead was at Apsley, but the geography and the existing development of the area made this impractical. The new main bus station was eventually built on the Two Waters site, as Jellicoe suggested. However it had always been his intention that this should stand next to a brand new railway station, so that the two main transport services could be most easily co-ordinated. What was termed an 'interchange' bus station was also to be built in the town centre and special regular 'star' services were planned to link the neighbourhoods with this station. The Master Plan noted that the airfield at nearby Bovingdon, then owned by the Ministry of Civil Aviation, had the potential to be used as an air terminal for the expanding New Town. This was in addition to the two helicopter pads which had already been prescribed for the town centre. Jellicoe had the foresight to suggest making more of the Grand Union Canal as a leisure amenity, but he also hoped to increase its economic use by building new wharves at Apsley.

The report to the 1947 Master Plan confirmed that the industrial area to the south-east at Apsley lay outside its designated area. However it stressed that this existing sector still remained an important part of the New Town infrastructure. In future, large scale industrial development was to be concentrated on a new site of 219 acres which was located at Cupid Green, to the north-east of the town centre. The plan confirmed that the neighbouring estate, then owned by the firework manufacturers, C. T. Brocks, would remain undisturbed. It also specified that the area immediately to the south of this, which contained existing clay workings on difficult contours, would be allocated for future use by extractive and semi-obnoxious industries. The new industrial zone at Cupid Green was to be spaciously planned, with the principal factories neatly located on either side of a specially constructed main road, which became Maylands Avenue. A further one hundred acres was to be retained for further expansion. In 1948 the Development

Corporation had already acquired some land to use as a camp for its labour force, when the first contract was awarded to Mowlem on 1st March 1948.

An amended Outline Plan and supporting report was presented to the Ministry of Town and Country Planning on 25th August 1949. It contained modifications to the proposals for the new housing areas. The residential property was now to be of four basic types, although only two types would account for 90% of the housing. Around one third of the houses to be built would have two bedrooms and just over half would have three. Importantly the 1949 plans included a revised scheme for the central area, with the earlier more ambitious plans for the town centre now amended in order to reduce the amount of demolition required. Shopping was now to be provided on both sides of Marlowes and the revised plan also provided more detailed schemes for car parking in the town centre. They allowed for an initial capacity of 750, with the majority of parking on the east side of Marlowes being either free standing tiered car parks or parking above retail units. The parking to the west of Marlowes was to be at ground level and integrated into the basic design of the Water Gardens. Running parallel to Marlowes, on the west side of the Water Gardens, would be the new Leighton Buzzard Road. This was being planned as the new through route northwards, avoiding the town centre. Marlowes itself would be one long straight road, approximately three quarters of a mile long. However some of the shops were to be positioned at right angles, providing a series of short additional pedestrian shopping ways.

The 1949 Report also reveals that the Development Corporation had given considerable thought to the need to create a socially balanced community. Because the town planners knew that the type of employment available in the New Town would largely determine the population mix, it was now considered essential to attract highly skilled white-collar industries which would attract a fair proportion of middle income groups. The report also acknowledges that the existing town was deficient in service industries and related social amenities. Partly for this reason, and to help build a community spirit, the Development Corporation was now anxious to develop some recreational buildings in the central area. A medium sized hall for meetings, dances and social gatherings was identified as a priority in the 1949 Report, but this was one key objective that was to prove elusive until the 1960's. The Corporation also wanted to see at least one large hotel in the town centre, along with adequate provision of licensed premises in the neighbourhood areas.

Quite apart from first creating several distinct new neighbourhoods, which then still needed to feel they belonged to the New Town, the task facing the authorities was a very complex one. By the mid Twentieth Century Hemel

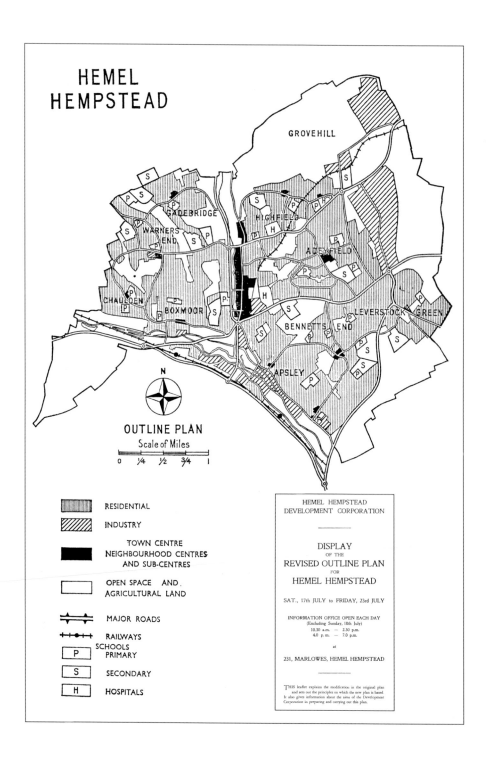

HEMEL HEMPSTEAD

GROVEHILL

GADEBRIDGE

WARNERS END

HIGHFIELD

ADEYFIELD

CHAULDEN

BOXMOOR

LEVERSTOCK GREEN

BENNETTS END

APSLEY

N

OUTLINE PLAN

Scale of Miles

0   ¼   ½   ¾   1

	RESIDENTIAL
	INDUSTRY
	TOWN CENTRE NEIGHBOURHOOD CENTRES AND SUB-CENTRES
	OPEN SPACE AND AGRICULTURAL LAND
	MAJOR ROADS
	RAILWAYS
P	SCHOOLS PRIMARY
S	SECONDARY
H	HOSPITALS

HEMEL HEMPSTEAD
DEVELOPMENT CORPORATION

DISPLAY
OF THE
REVISED OUTLINE PLAN
FOR
HEMEL HEMPSTEAD

SAT., 17th JULY to FRIDAY, 23rd JULY

INFORMATION OFFICE OPEN EACH DAY
(Excluding Sunday, 18th July)
10.30 a.m. — 2.30 p.m.
4.0 p.m. — 7.0 p.m.

at

231, MARLOWES, HEMEL HEMPSTEAD

THIS leaflet explains the modification in the original plan
and sets out the principles on which the new plan is based.
It also gives information about the aims of the Development
Corporation in preparing and carrying out this plan.

Hempstead had already grown into something of a fractured community, comprising three almost independent areas which socially had little to do with one another. The old town at the northern end of the Borough maintained a certain sense of historical superiority and distance from the rest of the community. Apsley was essentially an industrial suburb born out of the paper industry at the beginning of the Nineteenth Century, whilst Boxmoor was a white collar commuter area which had grown up around the arrival of the London to Birmingham railway in 1837. It was all these factors which, some years later, led Mr. Gilbert Hitchcock, the town's first Labour Mayor to comment that the moulding of Hemel Hempstead New Town "was one of the biggest pieces of social engineering this country has ever seen".

Given the difficult topography common to all the residential areas, and also the large amount of land required for suitable sites, the planning of secondary schools was proving difficult. It was clear from the 1949 Report that these would now need to be provided partly on grouped sites and partly as individual schools. The plan was that Apsley, Bennetts End and Leverstock Green would initially be served by one school. There would be a secondary school at Adeyfield and another at Highfield, which would also serve the northern part of the town. A further two schools would cater for Boxmoor, Warners End, Chaulden and the rest of the town centre area. Sites for a college of education had been reserved at the north end of Marlowes and it was confirmed that there was adequate provision of land to cater for the religious needs of the community. The existing cemetery at Cotterells Hill was to be retained and an attractive site at Leverstock Green was also being reserved in case additional capacity should be required.

The 1949 amendments to the original 1947 Master Plan were themselves modified in the light of the Minister's observations and also the results of a Public Inquiry which opened on 15th November 1949. The revised plan was eventually published in September 1951 and received its final approval in June 1952. The approval of this document was now sufficient to legislate for a ten year period of New Town construction at Hemel Hempstead. By 1960, and at the request of the Minister, the Development Corporation was already working with the County and Borough Councils on a second Master Plan to show how the town could be expanded further from 60,000 to 80,000 inhabitants. Its principal recommendation was the construction of 2,800 dwellings in the Grove Hill area which would, by themselves, accommodate another 9000 people. The new plan was subject to its own public inquiry held on 31st January 1961. The Government's sanctioning of this further plan was a clear indication that Jellicoe's original vision for the New Town, built around the neighbourhood principle, was officially considered a success.

Building a New Town

House building for the New Town began in 1949 and Adeyfield was the first neighbourhood to be developed. Construction work in this initial stage involved 415 dwellings, fourteen shops, a junior school and an infant school. In a special ceremony on 23rd April 1949, the Mayor and Bailiff of Hemel Hempstead, Councillor A. L. Selden, laid the foundation stone for the first house. Essential services, roads and sewers had already been built in advance, when the first release of funding became available in 1948. The Development Corporation had officially acquired 560 acres of land for construction and in 1949 confirmed the compulsory purchase orders, which were necessary to clear away some of the old properties in Marlowes, on land intended for the new central shopping area. The main road for the new industrial area was already under construction in 1949 and the first factory was being built. Appropriately, the industrial estate's first new tenant was the Hemel Hempstead Engineering Company, a local company who had relocated from the old town. The financial implications of building a New Town were now beginning to make themselves felt; in the first twelve months construction contracts worth £872,000 had been awarded and total capital expenditure to date had reached £476,000.

Advanced plans for the provision of all main services to the town were already well in hand. A reservoir at Adeyfield, with a three million gallon capacity, was 30% complete and in 1949 work had begun on the new Gade valley trunk sewer, supervised by the Colne Valley Sewerage Board. This was a key element of the early New Town construction work because, until it was completed in 1953, the speed of the residential settlement was limited by the capacity of the existing sewerage works. By 1950 a scheme for mains water supply had been agreed with the Borough Council and a new well was completed at Piccotts End. This new well would be able to provide the estimated 4.5 million gallons of water a day that the New Town would eventually require. The British Electric Authority addressed their need to enlarge capacity by building a major transformer station at Piccotts End and an outline scheme had been agreed with the Watford and St. Albans Gas Company for mains gas supply. A twelve inch main had already been provided from London Road, Apsley to Elephant Farm in the Bennetts End area. An outline plan was also confirmed with the Post Office, who by now had supplied sufficient telephones and distribution lines to cope with the immediate development. By early 1951 the Post Office had established their new temporary exchange buildings at St. Albans Road, close to what was to become the southern end of the new town centre.

The New Town's first tenants moved into Homefield Road, Adeyfield in February 1950. In November of that year Lord Reith left the Board of the

Lord Reith speaking at the stone laying ceremony for the first house at Adeyfield, 23rd April 1949.

'L' type houses under construction in Windmill Road, Adeyfield, April 1950.

Hostel for construction workforce, Adeyfield, 1949.

Building work in progress on the 3 million gallon reservoir at Adeyfield, 19th July 1951.

Development Corporation and the Corporation's Report, published in 1951, acknowledged the significant role he had played helping to establish the New Town movement. By the Spring of 1951, 292 houses had been completed and fourteen shops at Adeyfield were ready for business. The first primary school opened in January, with a second already under construction. In 1951 the process of development was accelerating rapidly with a total of 1264 acres of land now acquired for construction. The sum of capital expenditure totalled £2,000,000, whilst the value of New Town construction contracts awarded had risen to £3,000,000. The total workforce had grown from an initial 400 to over 1000 employees and the Corporation's initial target of 750 flats and houses completed was comfortably exceeded by 50 dwellings by the end of 1951. The 1000th New Town house at Hemel Hempstead was completed on 23rd April 1952 and was officially opened by Ernest Marples MP, Parliamentary Secretary of the Ministry of Housing and Local Government. The Development Corporation had already enjoyed considerable success, achieving the highest new housing figure for any New Town being built in Britain. The one thousand dwellings at Hemel Hempstead represented about a quarter of the total housing stock which had then been built by all twelve New Towns in England and Wales. By the end of the financial year 1951/52 the Corporation had also built 12 miles of roads and 28 miles of sewers for the New Town.

At Adeyfield 3000 people had already moved into dwellings provided by the Corporation, increasing the population of the area to 4,500 by the end of March 1952. There was now a need to press on with the second stage of development at Bennetts End and Apsley, where plans to cater for a further 9000 people on a site of 820 acres had received their final approval on 26th June 1951. By April 1952 houses were being completed at a rate of two dwellings per day and the total labour force had risen from 1000 to 2000 construction workers. It became necessary for the Development Corporation to enlarge its hostel at Adeyfield, which could now accommodate up to 440 labourers. The major programme of water works which included the new well and pumping station at Piccotts End, a rising main and the large reservoir at Adeyfield was operational by October 1952. By this time the high pressure gas main had been extended through Bennetts End to Leverstock Green, with a spur added to provide service to the industrial area. The highlight of 1952 was an official visit by Her Majesty Queen Elizabeth II, who came to Adeyfield on 20th July to lay the foundation stone for St. Barnabas Church. After a service on the site of the church, she toured both the Adeyfield and Bennetts End neighbourhoods and also inspected progress on the new industrial area. In 1952 the Borough Council had succeeded in purchasing the estate of Gadebridge Park and fully intended to preserve part of it as a central public open space for the New Town.

The new tenants await the official opening of the 1000th house, 23rd April 1952.

Harold Macmillan attends the opening of the 2000th house, 23rd March 1953.
Also showing (left to right) Henry Wells, Viscountess Davidson and Charles Kirk.

Her Majesty Queen Elizabeth II visits Adeyfield, 20th July 1952.

Most of the incoming population to Hemel Hempstead tended to be young, with a particularly high proportion of children under five, and consequently two and three bedroomed houses tended to be in greatest demand. A growing number of school children at Bennetts End were having to be accommodated at Adeyfield, until their new school would be ready in 1953. The town planners had the delicate job of balancing the amount of building for houses with that of shops and services, schools and factories. In particular there was a concern that if factories were not built fast enough, Hemel Hempstead would become more of a dormitory town. The availability of good quality employment was also important in terms of attracting and retaining a skilled and youthful population. There was of course no shortage of work locally for those involved in the construction industry, many of whom became some of the Corporation's first tenants.

On 23rd March 1953 the Rt. Hon. Harold Macmillan MP, Minister for Housing and Local Government, visited the New Town to open the 2000th house to be completed. Work was forging ahead and new homes at Hemel Hempstead were now being produced at a rate of over 1000 per year. The town's population had already grown by 6,500 and the Development Corporation's expenditure on construction work alone had now risen to £4 million per annum. New mains for gas, electricity and water were being laid throughout the New Town area at the impressive rate of one mile per month. During the year a total of 369 street lamps were erected in new streets. Building work was now concentrated in Bennetts End with 1200 dwellings under construction; 1953 also saw the beginning of work on the Chaulden neighbourhood where 414 houses were completed. The main phase of work at Adeyfield was now drawing to a close. A further thirteen shops had been added in the central square and the New Town's first public house, 'The New Venture' was already open. At Bennetts End the first group of shops was now also open for business and work was underway on the 'Golden Cockerel' public house and a second primary school for the area, as well as a secondary modern school and a grammar school.

The Development Corporation's report dated March 1954 was able to declare that new residents were arriving in the town at the rate of ten per day and, as a result, a substantial level of income was now starting to accrue from the new tenants. At this still relatively early stage, for every £10,000 spent on either land acquisition or construction, £1200 was already being recovered in income. A confident Corporation submitted plans to the Ministry for a further three year period, from 1954 to 1956, aiming to provide new housing at the rate of 1200 dwellings per annum. Now that the industrial area and principal neighbourhoods to the west had been established, the focus of activity was switching to the east and the development of new residential areas at Chaulden, Warners End and Gadebridge. The greater part of

Warners End had already been planned in detail and building work started there at the end of 1953.

The 15 inch water main for Bennetts End was completed in 1953 and the 24 inch Boxted trunk main was operational as far as Warners End by May 1954. This key achievement meant that lack of water supply was no longer a limiting factor in the development of the western neighbourhoods. The Eastern Gas Board had already been successful in laying distribution mains well in advance of house completions, and the Eastern Electricity Board had so far managed to meet all demands for additional supply. The completion of the A414 St Albans Road enabled the Post Office to lay new telephone trunk lines connecting the town with St Albans. In 1954 the Corporation had also constructed Combe Street and Waterhouse Street, the first new streets in the town centre. By 1955 work had started on the five million gallon capacity Boxted reservoir, which was designed to serve the modern neighbourhoods. This year the Corporation also completed a connecting road between Warners End and the town centre. The population of the town had now reached 38,500 and by 31st March 1955 a total of 4164 dwellings had been completed by the Corporation. Water consumption had now reached 2.3 million gallons per day, which was already more than double the amount previously consumed by the old town. At this stage the Chaulden neighbourhood was half finished and Warners End was the main scene of extensive building activity. In addition plans for the Gadebridge area and the northern half of the Highfield neighbourhood had now been approved by the Minister.

Later in the year preliminary works to open up the Gadebridge neighbourhood were started. At this early stage the Corporation was finding it difficult to dispose of flats which accounted for about 5% of the total housing stock. By April 1955 the rent roll of the New Town had reached £650,000, of which £115,000 was paid in rates. In 1955 former local teacher and Borough Councillor Wyndham Thomas became a Director of the Town and Country Planning Association. He was a leading influence in the development of the New Town and later served as a member of the Commission for the New Towns, before becoming the General Manager of Peterborough Development Corporation in 1968. The Hemel Hempstead Development Corporation's General Manger since its inception, Mr. W. O. Hart, had resigned in January 1956 to become Clerk to the London County Council and Brigadier G. B. S. Hindley C.B.E. was appointed in his place. The Brigadier inherited a New Town project which had already received a total investment of £18 million and this was scheduled to reach £24 million by 1958. The most visible development in 1956 could be seen in Marlowes where the central shopping area had been established. In June 1955 an important and symbolic part of this process had been the transfer of the town's market from its old High Street site to the new square provided for it in Marlowes. At the southern end of the town, on land provided by the Corporation, the Town Council built the Plough roundabout at a junction which had been struggling to cope with the intersection of five increasingly busy roads. As part of its contribution to town centre traffic developments, the Corporation later built a twin carriageway running from this roundabout to the southern end of the new shopping area.

By 1957 the population of Hemel Hempstead had reached 44,800 and there was now a total of 11,300 employment opportunities provided by local factories and employers. The impressive speed of this achievement within the first eight years, does not mean that there were not significant planning problems in the early days of the New Town development. Rising costs of building, increased borrowing rates and several post-war economic crises, had gradually combined to reduce the standard of housing and also increase the rents required. Furthermore the funding restrictions introduced by central Government had reduced the speed of road building. They also prevented many of the planned social amenities from being available to the early New Town community. Another ongoing problem was the provision of primary school places which always threatened to fall behind the growing needs in the new neighbourhoods. With young families most attracted to the New

New Park Drive, Adeyfield, 1954.

Early view of Marlowes, close to Market Square, circa 1957.

Town, the age structure of the population had become very different from the national average. Even when allowance was made for the national post-war baby boom, it was already obvious that Hemel Hempstead would have an unusually high number of children per capita to be educated throughout the next generation.

The financial year 1957/58 was an important year for religious developments. Two Church of England churches, St Alban's at Warners End and St Benedict's at Bennetts End, were opened. The Roman Catholic church of St Mary the Virgin was built close to the St Albans Road and a Baptist church at Gadebridge were also completed during the year. An important strategic advance in the development of the New Town occurred when work began in July 1958 on a link road to the newly constructed London to Birmingham motorway. The industrial estate's connection to the nation's first motorway would prove to be an essential part of Hemel Hempstead's future economic health and prosperity. The Corporation had now rationalised its programme of house building according to grades. Properties designated Grade I were terraced houses, available for weekly rent, which were being built at a density of 12-15 per acre. Grade II were semi-detached houses with garages built at 7-9 houses per acre, whilst Grade III were larger semi-detached or detached houses, with a garage provided, at 5-7 per acre. The proportion of

Aerial view of the first major factories built on the Industrial Estate at Maylands Avenue, June 1957 (Wood Lane End, bottom left).

graded properties built favoured a cheaper, denser housing mix, with the planners aiming at 75% Grade I, 20% Grade II and only 5% Grade III houses. In 1959 it was confirmed that the New Town had now become self supporting. The Corporation had a total of 7,066 weekly tenants, producing a surplus on the general revenue account of £56,000 at the end of the financial year 1958/59. Up to this point the total cost of the New Town development had been £26 million and the population of Hemel Hempstead had expanded from 22,000 in 1947 to just over 50,000 inhabitants.

In early 1959, a total of 700 houses had been completed in Gadebridge and the shopping centre was nearing completion. Queen Elizabeth, the Queen Mother, visited the town on 14th July 1959 to open a new wing of the West Herts Hospital. This local hospital's continued existence near to the town centre had earlier been threatened by Jellicoe's original Master Plan. Another significant visit had occurred on 18th April 1959 when Henry Brooke MP, Minister for Housing and Local Government, had officially opened the new community hall at Bennetts End. It had become apparent during the year that the child population in the western sectors of Warners End and Gadebridge was increasing at an even faster rate than the earlier neighbourhoods. This necessitated a further review of school provision, as a result of which it was decided that a Roman Catholic school should be built on a site to the north-west of the town. A new concern was the growing demand for old persons dwellings from the elderly relatives of Corporation tenants. By 1960 a total of 525 old persons dwellings had been built, but there was already a lengthening waiting list for a further 364 places.

Exceptionally bad weather in 1960 hampered the progress of house building. The next area due to be developed was Highfield, which was located directly opposite Gadebridge in the north-eastern sector of the town. Despite the difficulties that winter, 123 houses were still completed at Highfield and a start was made on the neighbourhood centre in October 1960. The town planners adopted a fresh modern approach for the Highfield area, which was designed to ensure most of its residents greater privacy and freedom from road traffic. This was achieved despite a relatively high density of housing in the area. Also in 1960 work began on the last neighbourhood for which the Corporation was to be responsible. This was at Leverstock Green, which had long been planned to be a much slower and careful development around an existing village green and rural style community. The majority of building at Leverstock Green was to comprise better quality housing, much of which was to be developed by private enterprise. In 1960 work had also started on a small development at Longdean Park which offered 112 plots, reserved for higher quality housing.

At the start of the 1960's there was evidence of increasing interest in house purchase. Renting was no longer the automatic option for so many families and by the Spring of 1960 the Corporation had already sold 67 of its own formerly rented properties. Another feature at the beginning of the decade was the dramatic spread in car ownership. When construction work on the New Town had begun, ten years earlier, the Corporation was permitted to build garages at a rate equal to only 12.5% of the number of houses provided. By 1960 nearly 80% of residents moving to the New Town would have preferred a garage to be included with their new house. Another interesting feature was that some of the Corporation's earliest tenants had now reached marriageable age, and over 600 applications from these second generation young people were now swelling the demand for new housing.

Prompted by the spur road which linked Hemel Hempstead to the M1 motorway, the industrial area around Maylands Avenue had enjoyed rapid growth. The Trust House Forte Hotel was soon built off Breakspear Way, becoming the first hotel to be provided adjacent to a motorway in the United Kingdom. The New Town was also proving remarkably successful in attracting the decentralised offices of major commercial concerns and government agencies, that had previously been more expensively housed in London. In 1961 a total of 162,836 sq.ft. of office space had already been built, providing work for 820 office based personnel. A look back at the census

The Breakspear Motel, May 1965.

figures for 1951 indicate how successful the town planners had been in creating a more socially balanced and prosperous community for the fast expanding New Town. Within ten years the proportion of Class V unskilled residents in the town had plummeted from 14.7% to 5%, whilst those of Class 1 and II, professional and intermediate occupations had shown significant growth from 3.6% to 5.9% and 13.9% to 20.1% respectively.

Preparations were being made in 1961 for the dissolution of Hemel Hempstead Development Corporation and the transfer of its assets to the Commission for the New Towns. Due to its success, the Corporation was in the happy position of handing over a flourishing New Town that was now financially self supporting. At this point, despite the high level of immigration to Hemel Hempstead, and partly fuelled by the building boom, there was still more skilled employment opportunities than there were people to fill them.

However the pace of development had imposed heavy demands on the statutory authorities whose co-operation was required at all stages in the provision of essential services. The Corporation's entire sewerage system relied on the newly built Gade valley main outfall trunk sewer, which was now owned by the West Herts Main Drainage Authority. The town's sewerage system, built entirely by the Corporation, was transferred to the Borough Council on 1st April 1961. The responsibility for the water supply, which had been improved at the Borough Council's expense, was transferred to the Rickmansworth and Uxbridge Water Company on 1st January 1961. Prior to the New Town, Hemel Hempstead had been served by Watford Corporation's electricity supply from underground 11 kilowatt cables. In order to meet the increased demands of the New Town, the Eastern Electricity Board had installed a 132/33 kilowatt grid supply from a new distribution centre, built at Piccotts End. From this point several primary substations served the various neighbourhoods, via underground cables, providing a three phase 415 volt and 240 volt single phase supply throughout the town.

The first phase of supplying gas to the New Town had been the conversion of the low pressure North Watford to Boxmoor main to medium pressure, and the laying of a branch line to supply Adeyfield, Bennetts End and the industrial area. This was followed by the installation of a new main from Boxmoor which reinforced the town centre's supply and fed the new western neighbourhoods of Chaulden, Warners End and Gadebridge. More recent work by the Eastern Gas Board had followed the laying of another extension main to Highfield and the construction of a booster installation and a new gas holder of one million cubic feet capacity at Boxmoor.

Hempstead House, built over Marlowes in 1962, with the 'Waggon and Horses' (right).

Armourial Bearings of the Commission for the New Towns.

On 1st April 1962 the Development Corporation was replaced by the Commission for the New Towns. The population of Hemel Hempstead New Town was on target to reach 60,000 and the Corporation's job had been completed within 15 years from the date of the first Master Plan. By the end of 1962 a total of 13,214 houses had been built in Hemel Hempstead. In excess of ten thousand of these dwellings had been provided by the Development Corporation, 1,444 by the Local Authority and 1,314 had been privately built. With the majority of scheduled construction work already achieved, the role of the Commission for the New Towns was now to be mainly that of landlord. There was still more work to be done however, because a second Master Plan had been approved in 1961. This plan had been drawn up at the Ministry's request to show how the target population of 60,000 for Hemel Hempstead could now be increased to 80,000. The principal recommendation of this later plan was to provide an additional 6000 houses, many located in another brand new neighbourhood. This new residential neighbourhood was to be located to the north-east of the town at Grove Hill. The plan also specified some infilling of existing neighbourhoods and redevelopment work in the central area and at Apsley.

In 1962 a total of 629 new dwellings were completed, mainly at Highfield and Leverstock Green. By 1963 detailed plans for Grove Hill were well advanced and the design of the main drainage system was already in place. Most of the dwellings in the earlier neighbourhoods remained deficient in garages, but in future all new houses would have a garage included. The neighbourhood centre at Highfield, which comprised six shops, two surgeries, an estate office and a community hall had been completed by 1963. This brought the total number of shop premises provided in all the neighbourhoods of the

New Town to 129. During the year a Community Hall and Health Clinic opened in Warners End and plans were completed for a similar development at Gadebridge. By 31st March 1964 the population of Hemel Hempstead had reached 64,200 and was now expected to increase to 80,000 inhabitants by 1980. The Commission had completed a further 318 dwellings during the financial year 1963/64 and two 10 storey blocks of flats at Leverstock Green were nearly completed. The New Town now had a total stock of 531 old persons dwellings and in 1964 accommodation for a further 172 elderly people was being built for the Jewish Board of Guardians on land close to the town centre. Fifty-nine quality houses were being built by the Commission for sale in Chambersbury Lane, with prices that ranged from £4,650 to £5,500. The Commission for the New Towns was now happy to encourage self-build groups and negotiations were in hand for the disposal of up to four acres of land to various local co-operatives.

By 1964 work had started on the contract to provide wired television and radio for the town and a planning application had been submitted to site the master aerial at Bennetts End. Work at Highfield was drawing to a close and part of the design of this new neighbourhood had been commended by the Housing Ministry's Awards Committee. A total of thirteen new churches and places of worship had been provided for the New Town. Following reconstruction work the town's railway station at Boxmoor was officially re-opened in August 1964 and the building was renamed Hemel Hempstead Station. In 1964 the Commission had finally agreed to contribute over £8000 to the Borough Council towards the cost of a community centre at Gadebridge, work for which was now well advanced.

Early in 1965 rumours were circulating in Hemel Hempstead that tenancies of Commission dwellings were being obtained by irregular means. Following the conviction of a member of the Commission's local executive for the corrupt acceptance of money and for using false documents, the Commission decided to take legal steps to recover possession of these houses. Orders for possession were made against 87 tenants and these took effect between March and November 1966. In 1965 the Ministry had approved plans for a new neighbourhood centre at Leverstock Green and by 1966 construction work was beginning on the Grove Hill neighbourhood. The first area to be developed at Grove Hill was to contain 590 houses in a pedestrianised Radburn style layout, designed to keep residents segregated from road traffic. A total of 72 dwellings were to be provided for elderly people and 99 other properties were to be available for sale at prices ranging from £4,600 to £5,175. In general terms the scheme at Grove Hill was aimed at meeting demand for better quality housing. Although the rents were to be dearer there was to be a higher standard of both finish and amenity in this, the last official New Town development in Hemel Hempstead.

The first houses to be completed in Precinct A at Grove Hill were officially handed over to the respective tenants and purchasers by Robert Mellish MP, Joint Parliamentary Secretary to the Ministry, on 1st June 1967. The neighbourhood centre at Leverstock Green which included seven shops, a surgery, a hairdressing salon, eight dwellings with garages and a public car park was also completed during this year. In Autumn 1968 the town's High Street was revitalised by an overall 'face lift' jointly funded by the Civic Trust, the Commission for the New Towns, the Borough Council, Hertfordshire County Council and the High Street Association. By 1969 half the scheduled buildings in Precinct A at Grove Hill had been finished. The Commission for the New Towns had ceased to qualify for subsidy payments with which to finance future construction work and because of this, the demand for rented accommodation was now to be met primarily by the turnover of their existing housing stock. Partly as a result of this change, an ever closer working relationship was now being developed between the Commission and the Borough Council, especially in the housing sphere. Their joint housing list, first established back in 1964, was now catering for all the local housing needs, including those of the New Town's second generation.

All 595 dwellings in the contract for Precinct A at Grove Hill had been completed by the Spring of 1970. Work had also started on the main access roads to enable other areas of Grove Hill to be developed. In one of these areas the Borough Council planned to build another 675 dwellings. Hertfordshire County Council had already provided a local health centre for the area and the first phase of the Grove Hill neighbourhood centre, comprising a supermarket and nine commercial garages, was being built. A new public house, called 'The Cupid' was due to be opened on 1st April 1971 and by early 1972 Hemel Hempstead Borough Council had a total of 830 houses, either completed or under construction, at Grove Hill. During 1972 roads and services were provided for special sites in the neighbourhood, where various self help groups were being allowed to build 99 houses. The supermarket was now also open for business.

As the town moved towards completion, the role of the Commission was to adopt a different emphasis. Although still empowered by Parliament to complete some remaining development, and to provide limited financial assistance to the local authority, the Commission's principal objective was to enable the community to move towards municipal normality as soon as possible. The local authorities, with their considerable income and growing experience, were now expected to be able to take on full responsibility for services and statutory functions. In the future it was planned that the Commission, who already had much more limited powers than the former Development Corporation, would simply adopt a similar position to that of any other major property owner in the town. A late teething problem was

Some of the older buildings in Hemel Hempstead High Street following the rehabilitation work carried out in 1968.

Florence Longman House, completed in 1975.

Official opening of Florence Longman House on 21st September 1975; showing Gilbert Hitchcock and the Chairman of Dacorum District Council, Mr. J. Johnson.

that although the Commission's properties were comparatively modern, many lacked the range of fixtures and fittings that were now expected in the early 1970's. In particular there was a strong demand for improved heating systems. Unfortunately part of the response to this pressure led to a tragedy in one of the new flats in Grove Hill, where a gas fired and ducted warm air heating system had been installed. Contemporary reports indicate that the death of three occupants was partly attributable to defective air circulation and poor ventilation in the flat.

Positive efforts were now being made by the Commission to enable elderly occupiers to maintain their independence as long as possible, by providing some means of security. Four groups of elderly persons dwellings in the New Town were now linked by a speech warning system to wardens living in adjoining houses. By 1974 the Commission's first sheltered accommodation comprising 56 flats with two wardens living in attendance had been completed. One year later a second smaller scheme, Florence Longman House at Apsley, was ready for occupation and two other similar establishments were under construction. In 1975 the Commission's warden service, linked by a talk-back special alarm system, already covered a total of 572 dwellings for elderly people.

In 1974 the Commission's negotiations with a major national contractor for the development of the western sector of Grove Hill had ended in failure to reach an agreement. As a result of this, another 40 acres of land was made available to the Borough Council, with a further 21 acres being allocated to housing associations and self-build groups. Only 22 acres of land were now to be reserved for private development. The following year and subsequent to local government reorganisation in 1973, what was now Dacorum District Council immediately set to work building another 535 dwellings at Grove Hill. Early in 1975 four more shops were completed in the neighbourhood and work on an ecumenical Church and Community Centre was scheduled to start later in the year. During the financial year 1976/77, over 300 of the Council's 535 houses had already been completed and the development of the Grove Hill neighbourhood was drawing near to completion. Considering the speed of house construction during the first fifteen years of the New Town development, it may be surprising to realise that work had begun on this, the last of the New Town neighbourhoods, nearly ten years ago. In contrast to Adeyfield, which was a similar size and had been built in only four years, Grove Hill had been deliberately designed to grow at a much steadier rate than the earlier neighbourhoods. This was in order to help provide for the much slower and more natural expansion of the New Town that followed its peak period of growth during the 1950's and 60's. In this respect it was another example of finely judged town planning.

A Community Spirit

Much of the thinking behind the idea of a 'New Town', and the level of post-war social engineering it implied, was woven into the Greater London Plan, published in 1944. The principal recommendation made by the plan's author Professor Abercrombie, who was Knighted in 1945, was to rehouse many of the families who were struggling to exist in the already overcrowded residential areas of London. In short, this meant taking up to one million people from selected London boroughs and resettling them in a ring of brand new satellite communities which would be built to order around the Capital. The Boroughs of Acton and Willesden were eventually designated as the principal areas that would decant sectors of their population into the New Town to be built at Hemel Hempstead. Preliminary meetings held by the local authorities in these two boroughs indicated a willingness on the part of many people to positively consider such a move. Many of the younger families in particular, then living in these areas, were typically occupying only a couple of rooms in a large terraced house. These older properties were densely packed into what was very much an inner city environment. Most couples were therefore beginning their married lives with a very poor standard of basic amenities. With living space at a premium, washing space was limited and bathrooms uncommon. Many were still having to use an outside toilet and kitchens often amounted to no more than a shared cooker on a landing.

Recreational space in these inner city neighbourhoods was also non-existent. It is therefore not difficult to understand why the prospect of a brand new home in the Hertfordshire countryside seemed to offer the people of Acton and Willesden a tantalising glimpse of a much better life for themselves and their children. One newcomer is still adamant: "I was born in Willesden and a slum is a slum is a slum. I wouldn't go back to London, no blooming way!" Other early residents remember: "It was the best thing in our lives to see fields instead of soot and grime". "We used to visit friends in Hemel, but felt so depressed when we went back to our old home in Kilburn". "It was a clean tidy town and the Water Gardens were beautiful, after Willesden".

In the event the geographical spread of those moving out to the New Town at Hemel Hempstead covered a much broader area of north London. As the development began, enquiries were received from the Boroughs of Wembley, Harrow and Hendon, who were also prepared to provide some of the new population for Hemel Hempstead New Town. The Development Corporation became very proactive as they set about the task of attracting as many new young tenants as they could. Public relations was an important issue and the Corporation was naturally very keen to portray the project as a visible success, as soon as possible. To further this aim, the Development

Corporation funded the production of a promotional film called "A Home of Your Own" which was first shown at the Festival of Britain in 1951. The film was also financed to run in two major West End cinemas for a three week period that summer. This advertising feature, which confidently outlined the attractions of life in the New Town at Hemel Hempstead, was then shown at a further 100 cinemas throughout the London area, and at over 150 other outlets in the outer London area during the year.

The age profile of those who first arrived in the New Town from 1950 was heavily weighted to those with young families. Consequently there was an immediate and pressing need for the development of educational provision in all the new neighbourhoods. Allowance was also to be made for designated play areas with special equipment provided. However not everybody was keen on youngsters playing on the streets and letters in the first of the community newspapers, the 'Adeyfield Argus', complained about the noise and mess made by the new hordes of young children enjoying themselves. A forerunner of the current adventure playground scheme was the idea to create 'junk play areas' for the children. These utilised drain pipes, planks and other surplus building materials, but met with limited success. Even in these early days, the Development Corporation had the foresight to realise that there would eventually be a similar bulge in the elderly

Early residents moving into their new house.

population. In anticipation of this, they began a phased programme of building bungalows and flats for the elderly in 1955. By 1959 they had completed over 300 such dwellings in five different neighbourhoods.

In direct contrast to the inner city environment that many of the newcomers were used to, the design of the new neighbourhood areas aimed to reduce the amount of straight line construction, improving the view from the windows. When planning to accommodate large numbers of people in what were still relatively small areas, the town planners and architects worked hard to avoid monotony. Each individual neighbourhood was given its own distinctive design features and a wide variety of architectural styles and construction materials were employed to break up the harshness and conformity of plain brick walls. The need for both colour and the development of originality was encouraged in many different ways. One of the most successful of these early initiatives was the establishment of local gardening clubs. Given the enthusiasm of many people who had never had a garden before, this often produced spectacular results.

The first tenants officially chosen to move into Hemel Hempstead New Town were Mr. Ben Adams and his family at 6 Homefield Road, in Adeyfield. However the first occupants to actually move in were the Ellerby family next door. The keys were handed to them on Wednesday, 8th February 1950 in the presence of the Mayors of Acton and Willesden. Representatives were also present from both Harrow and Wembley, two more boroughs that were to provide many of the early tenants. To help people settle in, the Development Corporation provided such publications as 'Welcome to Hemel Hempstead' and 'Getting to Know Hemel Hempstead' and these were distributed free to all new residents. From 1950 Mrs. Penny, the Housing Manager, was also on hand to greet the new arrivals, many of whom could scarcely believe their luck: "A new house, even in the back of beyond, was wonderful after our bomb damaged flat in Cricklewood". Compared to their previous homes, many thought they had "arrived in paradise", when they saw their brand new home with all its facilities. One grateful newcomer remembers "It was a wonderful house, an inside toilet with our own bath, a proper kitchen and a garden. Cavity walls to keep us warm and a lovely view from the windows". There could be no doubt that children's lives were also transformed by the move to the New Town. Growing youngsters now had green space to run around in and could breathe fresh country air, often for the first time in their lives.

However the early days were not without their share of difficulties. In particular matching the number of houses in any one area to the services available was not an easy task for the town planners. For example, local shops could not be opened until there was enough of a resident population

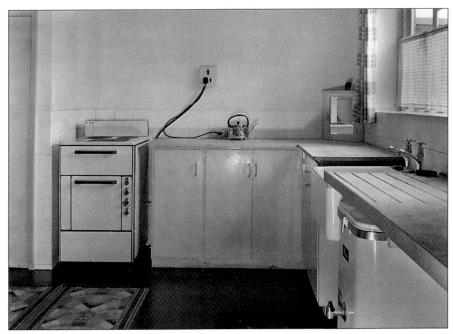

The kitchen of a newly completed house at 29 Longlands, Adeyfield.

The lounge of 29 Longlands, Adeyfield.

Topping-out ceremony in Windmill Road.

Topping-out celebrations.

to make the enterprise viable. Many young mothers at first faced a long trek into town, often through hazardous and unpleasant building sites. However it was possible to buy basic provisions from the Co-op mobile service and Express Dairy vans that regularly toured the expanding neighbourhoods. A distinctive feature of the early New Town houses was that they were all provided with a Marley tile floor throughout, which was unfortunately rather difficult to keep clean. Because most people had moved out of London with very little money, the standard of furnishing inside the houses was, by necessity, very spartan at first. Some of the first tenants rushed headlong into expensive hire purchase agreements, so that they could quickly provide new furniture and fittings to go with their brand new house. Some older residents still remember the 'Tally men', who would call on a weekly basis to collect these hire purchase payments.

The early settlers also faced difficulties whilst there were still unmade areas around their houses. With such a heavy programme of construction work going on all around them, in wet weather everything turned into a sea of mud. Where possible long planks were laid between the houses and the nearest available road surface, but mud soon oozed up between them. One of the first housewives remembers: "There was so much mud when you first came here, Oh my God!". Certainly young couples moving into their new house were not short of advice. The Borough Council's Tenants Handbook was full of handy hints such as "your post war house at Hemel Hempstead lends itself excellently to the homely and cheerful white net curtain, especially if the housewife really spreads herself and adds a few frills upon them!". Tenants were also advised that their WC "was not meant to take rags, old floor cloths, tins or large quantities of paper and care must be taken not to choke it".

There was very much a pioneering spirit, both amongst the building workers, many of whom were some of the New Town's first inhabitants, and the early groups of residents in the neighbourhoods. As a new house was finished and ready for occupation, a 'topping out' ceremony was often performed by the workers who had completed it. This usually involved the placing of a flag or broom on the chimney top. When the first house in Windmill Road, Adeyfield was completed a barrel of beer was used, which certainly added to the mood of the festivities! The community spirit often started on the very first day, with neighbours helping each other to settle in. Some of the older residents in Hemel Hempstead have written moving reminiscences which speak of the instant and lasting friendships which began in those early days: "From that day to this, my dear next door neighbour was the best friend I ever had". In some cases, nearly fifty years later, the same social groupings continue to live side by side in the original neighbourhood areas.

Of course not everyone was happy. There was inevitably going to be a proportion of the new population who would find it impossible to adjust to the new style of life. Some missed the bustle and excitement of the inner city and felt that they had no choice but to return. Famously one person, who clearly had never strayed far from London, complained bitterly about being woken early in the morning by "the noise them bloody birds made!". Another ongoing problem of the early days is illustrated by the memories of one couple who recall going to the chapel on their first Sunday morning in Hemel Hempstead. "The minister was preaching about tolerance; how everyone must tolerate the newcomers to the town! This was the first time that we realised that we might not be welcome here". Certainly there was some bad feeling from some of the elderly townspeople in particular, who resented the rash of modern shops and offices which had so transformed the original look of Marlowes. As you would expect, there was also some widespread disapproval of the new large housing estates which had swallowed up so many of the rolling green fields previously surrounding the old town. One newcomer has since written with feeling on this attitude: "The old town people hated the New Town and all the people in it, "these Londoners" they used to call us". However following a decade of development, the improvement in economic prosperity brought by the New Town development was obvious to all but the most obstinate. By 1961 G. Brooke Taylor, the Development Corporation's Public Relations Officer, was able to write how "although the task of constructing a New Town could have originally been viewed as the imposition of an alien population on a small and already distinct community, it has now come to be recognised by most people locally as an enlargement and redevelopment which is steadily benefiting not only the new, but also the original inhabitants". Gerry Brook Taylor, who served as the Public Relations Officer for the Development Corporation from its inception in 1947 until 1962, played a leading role in helping to smooth the development of the New Town. He was awarded an OBE in 1967.

In order to help foster the success of the New Town, the Development Corporation was naturally very keen to do what it could to help build a community spirit and it appointed officers to initiate developments in this area. It was they who helped create the first community associations in the new neighbourhoods and also encouraged the beginnings of various local newsletters. The Adeyfield Argus and the Bennetts End Bugle, published from 1952 and 1953 respectively, were the longest running neighbourhood newspapers. Other examples of these important publications were the Chaulden Post (from 1956) and the Warners End Web (from 1957). The squeeze on funding had hindered the provision of even basic social amenities in the first few years. As a consequence of this, the need for central meeting points and social venues in the neighbourhoods was often met by re-using

Chambersbury Lane, November 1953.

Peascroft Road on the corner of Kier Ground, Bennetts End, 1954.

Meeting of the Adeyfield Neighbourhood Council.

Dancing in Adeyfield Hall, 1954.

some of the old discarded builders huts. The first such hall was provided for the community association at Adeyfield. These sheds were redecorated by the residents themselves to become a venue for local social occasions and dances. They also acted as an early community centre where local organisations could hold their meetings.

Sites for permanent halls had been reserved in the initial planning of the neighbourhoods, even though it was known that the actual buildings could not be provided at the outset. As far back as 1954 the Development Corporation had discussed the provision of a public hall in the new town centre itself, but the town council decided that it could not then afford to help finance such a building. By 1955 the Hemel Hempstead Council of Social Service had been joined by representatives of the Adeyfield and Bennetts End Neighbourhood Councils. These early neighbourhood councils played a valuable role by voicing local opinions on particular problems as the New Town development work continued. The voluntary efforts of the newcomers and their contribution to the community was impressive; already over sixty organisations had sprung up which covered most forms of social and cultural life. The Corporation had done its best, within the financial limits set, to provide some form of meeting place in all the neighbourhoods so far established. When Lord Reith spoke at the official opening of the first permanent community hall at Adeyfield on 31st October 1953, he was particularly scathing about the Government's continuing inability to produce the funding required to create a social infrastructure, as and when the new neighbourhoods were being built. Several years later there was still widespread recognition that not enough was being done. The Corporation's Annual Report in 1957 stated unequivocally that "there can be no satisfaction until each neighbourhood had its own permanent structure where committee meetings and entertainments can be held".

In 1958 the New Town of Hemel Hempstead, which was also celebrating its Diamond Jubilee as a Borough, held its first Festival of Arts. This festival was sponsored by the Development Corporation and proved to be an outstanding success. Local art, photographic and film groups organised a series of exhibitions and there were lectures by distinguished celebrities. Impressive musical concerts and top class drama were bought to the New Town for the first time during a hectic week in September. The festival proved so popular that it became an annual event thereafter. Following these successful arts festivals the Borough Council decided that a permanent Arts Trust should be established for the town. Alderman Gwen Marshall played a leading part in expanding the Festival Society into an Arts Trust and in 1960 she became the first female Mayor of Hemel Hempstead. The Trust's role was to foster and promote local interest in music and the visual arts, drama, poetry and other cultural activities. The Chairman of the Arts Trust for ten years was Mr. Henry Aughton. Having served as Borough Treasurer for fourteen years, Mr. Aughton played a significant role in local affairs. He was also selected to become the first Chief Executive of the newly formed Dacorum District Council, following the local government reorganisation of 1973.

Despite these successes a profile of Hemel Hempstead in the Daily Mail of 14th August 1961 pointed out one significant outstanding social problem in the New Town. Although it reported that most of the newcomers were happy in their new setting, the local teenagers "longed for the excitement of modern ballrooms and bowling alleys". The national newspaper declared that "the town was dead after seven o'clock at night and there is nothing for anyone in the housing estates". It was certainly true that by 1960 the unusual age structure of the town accentuated the lack of provision of leisure facilities for the youth of Hemel Hempstead. As an example of the exponential growth in this sector of the population, the numbers of teenagers in the town had grown from 500 in 1952 to over 4000 only five years later. The Development Corporation was deeply concerned about the shortfall in facilities and had begun working with other interested parties to try to tackle this issue. Most of the community buildings in the neighbourhoods were dominated by adult activities, with some use made of the makeshift halls by local cub and brownie packs and other clubs for younger children; the teenagers were effectively being squeezed out. In the course of time it was hoped to transfer the use of these existing buildings to local youth clubs, once the money was available to provide more permanent community centres in each of the neighbourhoods.

In the town centre the Corporation decided to convert an old building, close to the Princess Cinema, which became the 'Hi-Fi Youth Club' in Marlowes. In 1960 the Hertfordshire County Council appointed a youth leader to support the development. However it was recognised that the provision of social amenities still fell considerably short of what was desirable in a town which had now grown to have a total population in excess of 60,000. Despite this it is interesting to note that, although in the early 1960's juvenile crime was a problem in Hertfordshire, its incidence in Hemel Hempstead remained consistently lower than the average elsewhere in the county. The Development Corporation had played a full part in the Town's Youth Advisory Committee, which was first established back in 1957. This forum united the County and Borough Councils, leading local industrialists and the Council of Social Service in a common endeavour to support the youth of Hemel Hempstead. Gilbert Hitchcock was appointed Chairman of the Youth Advisory Committee, where he worked tirelessly to improve facilities for young people. Councillor Gilbert Hitchcock became the first Labour Mayor of Hemel Hempstead in 1956 and was the youngest Councillor ever to serve

Theatre 'in the round' comes to Hemel Hempstead.

Hi-Fi Youth Club in Marlowes.

in this capacity. He was awarded the CBE in 1979. By 1962 there were three full time and two part time youth clubs operating in the town, with a combined membership of over 1000. In addition there were a further sixty organisations (scouts, guides etc.) attached to various churches in the town which boasted a further 2,800 members.

The Development Corporation Report, published in March 1962, informs that there were already over 200 adult social organisations or societies established in Hemel Hempstead, catering for all age groups with interests as diverse as archery, bingo and wine making. This is a good indicator of the general level of community spirit that had been achieved in the first twelve years of the New Town. Another factor which aided social cohesion and balance was that by now there was the beginnings of an elderly New Town population and some of the second generation Corporation tenants had began to marry and start families of their own in Hemel Hempstead. There was however no complacency at this stage and still much work to do. The final report of the Development Corporation is careful to note that "for a balanced life something more than housing, work and family unity is required". Seventeen years ago in Lord Reith's committee report it had been clearly stated that "the New Towns were to be developed as self contained and balanced communities, which were to be the very antithesis of dormitory suburbs".

In the New Town an impressive total of fifteen new churches or church halls had been built by 1963. In the early days many of these had to first operate from a garage or a hut; often sharing facilities with other denominations until their own church had been built. There can be no doubt that the Ministers of these churches and their assistants played a significant role in the running of most of the local neighbourhood councils. Quite apart from their prime function of catering for the spiritual needs of the local population, the new churches had been tremendously important. They acted as a much needed focal point of social support for many of the first residents, as they began their lives in the brand new neighbourhoods. In contrast to this, and perhaps surprisingly, the social role of the local public house seemed to decline in the New Town context. Although six new public houses had been built by 1963 in the various new neighbourhoods, prior to 1947 there had been no less than 55 licensed premises serving a town population of only 20,000. Fifteen years later the population of Hemel Hempstead, which had now grown 200% to 60,000, was catered for by only 48 public houses.

By 1964 the Hi Fi Youth Club, whose original buildings were demolished to make way for a new civic centre, had been re-established as the 1621 Club in brand new premises. These were provided by the Corporation at a concessionary rent for the next 21 years. Another bonus for young people

Bingo session at the Over 60's Club at Adeyfield Hall.

New Towns 'Star' Garden Competition winners, July 1955.

Ambassador Bowling Alley, 1971.

*Cycling event in the New Towns Festival of Sport held at Hemel Hempstead,
in September 1971.*

was that the building work on the Ambassador Bowling Alley had been completed in April 1963. With little competition, other than from the Odeon Cinema which opened in 1960, this was proving to be a very popular and commercially successful venue for teenagers to meet. Some 6,500 young people, between the ages of 16 and 21, were now members of local clubs and organisations.

The 1963 Festival of Arts was considered to be the most successful so far, with nearly 5000 people attending the various events and exhibitions. For the first time the Arts Trust had also arranged a Spring Festival which took place in March and April 1964. This featured mainly the work of local amateur artists. A much needed focus for cultural activities was now available in the shape of the new assembly hall which was part of the town's new college of further education. This had been built at the northern end of Marlowes in 1963. A little further south, also on the western side of Marlowes, work was now beginning on an impressive new building, close to the new Town Hall site, built by the Borough Council. This was to be called The Pavilion and would in future serve as the principal central venue for dances, concerts and other major social occasions in the town.

Sporting clubs, in particular soccer, rugby and cricket clubs, continued to grow. They found little trouble attracting additional support in the fast expanding New Town. The Hemel Hempstead Sports Development Council had been set up in 1963 and was soon overseeing a flourishing range of activities. As one example of this growth, by 1965 new cricket pavilions were being either built or planned by each of Hemel Hempstead, Boxmoor and Leverstock Green Cricket Clubs. The seventh annual New Town Festival of Sport was held in Hemel Hempstead in 1971. Seven New Towns were represented in a competition which featured a range of sporting events. At the end of the day, the host team finished a close second to the overall winners, Basildon.

By the time of its annual report of 1977, the Commission for the New Towns was confident enough to declare that facilities in the town centre were excellent and that there was now a strong community life in the New Town. Each neighbourhood now had its own neighbourhood association, representative of the various religious, social and political organisations. Furthermore levels of voluntary activity were high, with the local people themselves having successfully raised considerable sums of money towards the provision of social amenities in each neighbourhood. The Report declared that Hemel Hempstead was now a "successful union of new neighbourhoods, a town centre and an ancient centre in which a cohesive society has emerged".

Adeyfield

Adeyfield, the largest of the neighbourhoods created for the New Town of Hemel Hempstead, was also the first to be built. House building began in the area in 1949 and the initial contract for one hundred houses, featuring seven distinct designs, was awarded to the building firm of Jesse Meads in Chesham. In order to provide temporary accommodation for some of the construction workers, the Development Corporation erected some wooden huts at the end of Longlands. This was the beginning of what became known as the Adeyfield Hostel, which grew until it could accommodate over 400 people. This hostel was eventually closed and largely demolished in 1954, so that the site could be reused for new housing. A few of the more solid buildings left standing were later used as a Further Education Centre. The first properties to be built at Adeyfield were in Homefield Road and Longlands; the flats between Homefield Road and the St Albans Road were also part of the first phase of construction. The Chief Architect of the Hemel Hempstead Development Corporation, Mr. H. Kellett Ablett, was awarded the Urban Medal of the Eastern Housing Region for his early work in Adeyfield. In February 1950 the keys of four houses in Homefield Road were presented to the first new tenants in Adeyfield, each of whom were construction workers on the estate. One bricklayer and his family had been specially chosen from each of the four London Boroughs, then principally involved in supplying population for the New Town. Mr & Mrs Adams were from Wembley, Mr & Mrs Ellerby from Harrow, Mr & Mrs Neal from Acton and Mr & Mrs Fee from Willesden.

The fields of Coxpond Farm at Adeyfield were required for housing development and had been subject to a compulsory purchase order in 1948. The development of Old House Road and the Court area of flats, houses and bungalows for old people occupies the site of Adeyfield Farm. This particular farmhouse enjoyed the dubious distinction of being the first building to be demolished in the name of New Town development at Hemel Hempstead. The progress of building work in the early days of the New Town was rapid. By 31st March 1952 there were 4,500 people living in Adeyfield and the first fourteen shops in the neighbourhood's new shopping precinct had already opened for business in 1951. On 23rd April 1952 a house at No. 2 Haleswood Road was officially commemorated as the 1,000th New Town house to have been completed.

Adeyfield's first junior school, Maylands School, was also opened in 1952. This school, which later became Hobletts Manor, originally took its name from Maylands Woods. These were part of a belt of trees deliberately left undisturbed by the New Town planners, so they could help screen off the new neighbourhood from the industrial area being built further to the east.

ADEYFIELD ARGUS

NUMBER ONE SPONSORED BY THE ADEYFIELD NEIGHBOURHOOD COUNCIL **JUNE · JULY 1952**

The Neighbourhood Plan Takes Shape . . .

"Thats Our House" (Photograph reproduced by kind permission of "The Surveyor".)

Message from the Chairman of the Development Corporation

I am very glad of the opportunity of writing a few words in the first edition of the Adeyfield neighbourhood magazine. For one reason it enables me to wish this venture all success, for another it allows me personally to welcome the new residents of Adeyfield. Nor do I forget those who lived in the neighbourhood before the new roads, shops and houses were built, but who are now just as much a part of its life as those who have moved in.

The Corporation, of which I am Chairman, is responsible for developing a large part of the town. It is trying to do this as well as human ingenuity and the limitations of labour and materials will allow. The Development Corporation can, of course, only create the physical background to a community; the really important job must be done by the people who live in it, for the vitality and happiness of the community depends on them. An excellent start has been made, and I am sure that the " Adeyfield Argus " can help very much in the future, by introducing people to each other and to the many valuable organisations that are already established.

At the request of the people of Adeyfield, the Corporation has helped to launch this venture; I hope that soon it will no longer need that help and be as successful as it so well deserves to be.

HENRY W. WELLS.

In April, 1949, Councillor A. L. Selden, who was then Mayor of Hemel Hempstead, laid the first brick of the first house to be built at Adeyfield. Ten months later the first tenants moved in.

Now the 1,000th house has been occupied, and the new tenants, Mr. and Mrs. Richard Banks and their family, were welcomed by Mr. Ernest Marples, Parliamentary Secretary to the Minister of Housing and Local Government, on Wednesday, April 23rd.

Between the first house and the thousandth is the story of much achievement; an achievement which opens up new horizons for all the families who have moved to Adeyfield. There are bound to be a number of problems to be solved before the town settles down, and it is by the active co-operation of all concerned that this can be achieved.

(continued page 2, col. 1)

On Sunday 20th July 1952 Her Majesty the Queen paid an official visit to Adeyfield, in order to lay the foundation stone for the Church of St Barnabas. Following an open air service on the site of the Church, the Queen toured the neighbourhood and also visited the home of one of the New Town's first tenants, Mr & Mrs Ben Adams. It was the Adams family home which had also been used for some of the interior domestic shots used in the Development Corporation's promotional film 'A Home of Your Own' which was released in 1951. It was reported that the Queen had been particularly impressed by the modern and convenient kitchens provided in the new houses. Following this Royal visit the Corporation successfully sought permission to commemorate the occasion by naming the neighbourhood shopping area at Adeyfield 'The Queen's Square'. Prior to this Royal dispensation it had simply been known as 'The Square'.

A brand new public house was built for Adeyfield in the shopping precinct at Queens Square. 'The New Venture' opened its doors for the first time on Christmas Eve 1952. The pub's name had been chosen carefully to reflect the pioneering spirit of all those involved in the early days of New Town development. The inn sign featured an Elizabethan sailing ship venturing out into the New World. By early 1953 a further thirteen shops had been completed in Queens Square and work was also beginning on the construction of a milk distribution depot. Adeyfield Secondary School in Longlands was officially opened on 8th July 1953 by Sir Ronald Gould. In 1953 the first children's playground at Adeyfield was being prepared on the site between Homefield Road and Longlands. Local street parties to celebrate the coronation of Queen Elizabeth II were another feature of 1953. Also in that year, to commemorate Sir Edmund Hilary's conquering of Mount Everest, the local roads Everest Way, Tenzing and Hilary Roads were named; Sherpa Road was added much later in 1978. The new neighbourhood at Adeyfield now had a population of 6,000 people and over 30 local social organisations had already been established.

The focus for early social activity at Adeyfield was the Greenhills Club. Back in 1938 the Brocks Firework Company had provided a club house for their workers' Sports and Social Club. This was located adjacent to the Company sports field, on ground to the north side of Vauxhall Road. In 1948, when the Development Corporation acquired this land by compulsory purchase order, the facility was opened up to all those living in the new neighbourhood and the club renamed Greenhills. By 1951 the club had already built up a membership of over 400 and the club house also accommodated a branch library and local welfare clinic. Volunteers were building an extension to the premises and funding was being made available to help with the provision of two hard tennis courts.

The 'Square' at Adeyfield decorated for the Queen's visit.

Her Majesty Queen Elizabeth II meets the Neal family, 20th July 1952.

Interior of Greenhills Youth Club building.

Adeyfield School, 1954.

One and two bedroom flats, opposite Queens Square.

The New Venture public house, Adeyfield.

Adeyfield Hall.

Church service held in the Longlands Hut at Adeyfield in June 1952.

Local clubs and societies who required a smaller meeting place had been using the 'Longlands Hut', a low brick built building situated close to Adeyfield School. In 1952 all local organisations and interested parties formed themselves into the Adeyfield Neighbourhood Council, which was then able to represent all the various religious, social, political and trade interests active in the area. Again with the help of the Development Corporation, the Neighbourhood Council undertook the publication of the 'Adeyfield Argus', a bi-monthly magazine with an initial circulation of 2000. This important community newsheet survived to produce an impressive 48 issues over an eight year period 1952-1960.

Despite financial restrictions imposed by the Government, the Development Corporation responded to the need for a more permanent community building by providing Adeyfield Hall in the Queens Square. This new building was officially opened by Lord Reith on 31st October 1953. As the instigators of this scheme, the Corporation itself was responsible for financing and managing the hall, which featured a ballroom with a magnificent sprung maple floor. In order to comply with the Ministry's strict requirements that this new social amenity should pay its own way, it was necessary for the Corporation to arrange public dances and other events. The profits from such functions were then used to help keep the rents low for all the various voluntary organisations who were using the hall. Two rooms at Adeyfield Hall housed health clinics and an annexe was also provided for the local branch library, which opened on 2nd November 1954. Adeyfield Hall was the first community hall to be built for any New Town in England.

The Rev. Peter and Mrs Ann Stokes arrived in Adeyfield in 1951. Church services began in their drawing room at 4 Windmill Road and were later held in their garage which had been converted for worship. This became known as the St Faith's Garage Chapel and was blessed by the Bishop of St Albans on the 6th October 1951. As the congregation grew, services then moved to the hut at Longlands until the new church building was completed. These temporary arrangements became redundant when the Church of St Barnabas was finally dedicated by the Bishop of St Albans on 4th July 1953. The opening ceremony for Adeyfield's Congregational Church took place on 9th January 1954 and the foundation stone for the Hemel Hempstead East Roman Catholic Church was laid in October 1956. St Mary the Virgin, built on a site close to St Albans Road, was designed to serve the Catholic communities in Adeyfield and Bennetts End. This church, which has since been rebuilt as 'Our Lady Queen of All Creation', was officially dedicated by the Archbishop of Westminster on 19th October 1957.

Social developments continued apace and in 1954 the Greenhills Club had been converted into Adeyfield Community Association. It was now formally linked with the recently established Adeyfield Neighbourhood Council, with which it had helped found a local youth club, called 'Square One'. In 1954 Merryhill Nursery found a permanent home when it moved into Bennetts End House at the top of St Albans Road. An 'Over 60's Club' was also established in the same year, although it wasn't until 1958 that the neighbourhood's first old people's home was opened at Adeyfield Lodge. This was later followed by a second development in Southernwood Close, on the former site of Adeyfield House. Maylands School was now struggling to cope with the numbers of primary school children in Adeyfield, but this problem was eased when Broadfield Junior and Infant School opened in 1955. By 1956 the local population had grown to 8,000 and the Adeyfield neighbourhood was served by a total of six schools: one secondary, two junior, two infants and a private nursery.

The rapid growth of Adeyfield had made the provision of playing fields and recreation areas a necessity. The Development Corporation had initially laid out three areas intended as public open spaces and provided three football pitches, a cricket square and two tennis courts. The playing fields at Longlands, adjacent to Queens Square, provided the main facilities for the neighbourhood. These grounds were renamed Reith Fields, as an acknowledgement of the role Lord Reith had played in the development of

Church of St. Barnabas, Adeyfield.

Reith Fields, Adeyfield.

Classroom at Maylands School, Adeyfield, April 1951.

Two and three bedroom houses in Masons Road, Adeyfield, June 1952.

*Briery Way, Adeyfield. Mr. Kennedy mowing his grass and Mrs Kirk at her front door,
September 1954.*

the New Town. An announcement to this effect was made at the official opening of Adeyfield Hall and the old iron gates, from the former Boxmoor Foundry in Marlowes, were fitted as entrance gates to these fields at the rear of 'The New Venture'. For younger children the first of three adventure playgrounds for the New Town was established in Adeyfield at Turners Hill in 1972.

By the mid 1950's the main phase of construction work at Adeyfield had drawn successfully to a close. The area was described in the Development Corporation's annual report of 1956 as "probably the most complete New Town neighbourhood to be found in the Country". With its own newly built churches, public house, shopping centre, service industry, community hall, schools, old persons' dwellings and well equipped recreational areas it represented a model example of New Town planning. Today Queens Square remains the largest of Hemel Hempstead's neighbourhood centres, with 32 shops situated on three sides of the square. The buildings have continuous canopies with flats over and are of three storey construction. On the reverse side of the square is the public house which has now been renamed 'The Venture', with the Adeyfield Hall community centre close by. The opposite corner is dominated by the Church of St Barnabas, behind which is an impressive modern health centre called Everest House which opened in June 1985. A new church hall has since been added to St. Barnabas and this was blessed by the Bishop of St Albans on the 8th September 1991.

The square at Adeyfield is open, with an unusual triangular arrangement for car parking. An interesting feature can be found on the balcony of the flats in Longlands, overlooking the entrance to Queens Square. This is a representation of the Grant of Arms arranged for the New Town by Lord Reith in 1948. The shield contains the Tudor rose, signifying Hemel Hempstead's links with King Henry VIII. This rose is surrounded by a surveyor's chain which is intended to symbolise the activities of the Development Corporation, whilst the stag supporters at either side represent the County of Hertfordshire. The arms motto "Majora, Uberiora, Pulchriora," voices the hopes and aspirations of the New Town. Reith fields are adjacent to the shopping area and still provide an important focus of open space for the community. These playing fields and the Adeyfield School site are on either side of a pedestrian link to the Leverstock Green Road. The woods, playing fields and amenity space along High Street Green, near Briery Way, provide an important buffer between Adeyfield and the adjacent industrial estate. This particular stretch of woodland at Adeyfield still remains the most significant area of mature trees in the New Town area. To the south the A414 St Albans Road, which was extended to link into the New Town centre, effectively separates Adeyfield and the second neighbourhood to be built at Bennetts End.

Bennetts End

The estate of Bennetts End, built on an open plateau, was the second neighbourhood to be created for Hemel Hempstead New Town. The empty fields around Bennetts End Farm and Bennetts End House can be seen clearly on Nineteenth Century maps of the area. The only other significant feature on the local landscape, prior to the New Town development, was the old Isolation Hospital which was built off Bennetts End Lane. The Master Plan had specified that the new housing at Bennetts End was to be kept distinct by maintaining some open space for recreational use, which would separate it from the residential developments of the Corner Hall/Belswains area lower down the valley. Together with Apsley, these existing 'sub-neighbourhoods' were subject to their own share of redevelopment work as part of the overall New Town project. By the time of the Development Corporation's annual report in March 1951 the architect, Miss Judith Ledeboer, had produced comprehensive designs for the Bennetts End area which covered a total of 821 acres.

Construction work at Bennetts End began in late 1951. People started to settle into the neighbourhood during 1952 and, as building work progressed during the summer, the flow of new inhabitants increased rapidly. A temporary general store was opened in one of the first houses to be built in Candlefield Road. As an addition to the mobile Co-op and Express Dairy vans that toured the early neighbourhoods, this was one practical way of meeting the new inhabitants' basic needs, pending the completion of a local shopping centre. The first residents to move into the neighbourhood were the Stone family, who lived at 51 Bennetts End Road from April 1952. By the end of the year a population of 2,300 had already been established at Bennetts End. In December 1952 the Development Corporation purchased an old works canteen from one of the building contractors, to provide the first meeting hall for the new community. This building, which became known as the Candlefield Room, was also used for the first Church of England services to be held in the new neighbourhood. The provision of some recreational area, particularly for children, was now considered an urgent priority. In 1953 the Corporation responded to this need by providing five different play areas throughout the neighbourhood. The first fourteen shops in the newly constructed Bennetts Gate shopping precinct, which was built at the top of Barnacres Road, opened for business in early 1954.

Despite the fact that original plans for the New Town had placed particular focus on the Bennetts End neighbourhood being a centre for educational provision, the initial work on school development at Bennetts End did not proceed very smoothly. Construction work on the first junior school for the area was delayed by a freeze on new communal buildings, imposed on the

Bennetts Gate Neighbourhood Centre.

View of the terrace at Long John, Bennetts End, 1953.
Built by Wimpey to a design by Geoffrey Jellicoe & Partners.

Corporation by the Government in 1951. Hobbs Hill Wood School in Peascroft Road opened in May 1954 and another local primary school, Chambersbury, was completed in early 1955. Reddings Junior and Infant School, off Bennetts End Road, opened in January 1960 and this was followed by St Albert the Great RC School, built close to Rant Meadow, in 1962. As the numbers of young children continued to grow in the neighbourhood, an additional primary school was opened at Lime Walk in January 1974. In 1954 the secondary school at Adeyfield was open and all the older children from Bennetts End were at first taught there, until the new Apsley Grammar School and Bennetts End Secondary School were ready in September 1955. It was these two schools which subsequently merged in September 1970 to become Longdean School.

Bennetts End's own public house 'The Golden Cockerel', built as part of the neighbourhood centre, was open for business by Christmas 1954. In terms of social development, valuable lessons had already been learnt from earlier experiences at Adeyfield. In 1953 the Corporation provided three wooden buildings to act as a central meeting place and social venue for the new community at Bennetts End. These huts had previously been used in the town centre and were moved up to the neighbourhood, because the land they occupied was now required for part of the on-going redevelopment work in

The temporary shop of Mr. J. Smith in Candlefield Road, Bennetts End, 1953.

Local volunteers decorate Bennetts End Hall, September 1953.

Catering arrangements well in hand for the official opening of the temporary Community Hall at Bennetts End, September 1953.

Bennetts End Secondary Modern School.

Playground at Bennetts End, April 1954.

St Benedict's Anglican Church, Bennetts End, 1997.

The Roman Catholic Church of St Mary the Virgin, in Ritcroft Street,
prior to its demolition in 1985.

Original interior of the 'Golden Cockerel'.

Rear of Bennetts End Neighbourhood Centre.

Marlowes. This temporary community hall, which comprised one large hall and two smaller committee rooms, was opened by the Chairman of the Development Corporation, Henry Wells, on 19th September 1953. The newly formed Bennetts End Neighbourhood Council, established in March 1953, was quick to organise itself and by October had set up a management committee to administer the Hall. The annual report of the Development Corporation of 1954 stated that although the Bennetts End neighbourhood was "still in the pioneering stage, social activities are well developed". The 'Bennetts End Bugle', a bi-monthly magazine run by the Neighbourhood Council, was already well established. In addition to a range of activities for adults, the Bennetts End Neighbourhood Association, established in April 1954, was also running a local youth club in one of these three meeting rooms.

By 1953 sites had been agreed for the provision of several places of worship to serve the Bennetts End community. The Baptist Church at Bennetts End officially opened on 18th June 1955 on its present site in Belmont Road; prior to this the church had been housed in a temporary builders hut from 25th January 1953. The Wesleyan Methodist Church in Bennetts End Road first opened its doors in July 1956 and this building is now used by the Seventh Day Adventist Church. The foundation stone of the St. Benedict Anglican Church in Peascroft Road, was laid on the 12th May 1956 and, following a series of delays, was consecrated by the Bishop of St Albans on the 8th February 1958. The foundation stone for the Roman Catholic Church of St Mary the Virgin was laid by Bishop Craven on 28th October 1956. The blessing and official opening of this church in Ritcroft Street, which was designed to serve the Catholic communities in Bennetts End and Adeyfield, was attended by the Archbishop of Westminster one year later on Saturday 19th October 1957. Unfortunately this building suffered from structural problems which necessitated its demolition in 1985. A new church, Our Lady Queen of All Creation, was built on the same site and re-opened on 13th November 1987. At the top end of the neighbourhood, in an area next the Catholic Church, local street names such as Bricklayers Lane, Brickfield and Tile Kiln Lane are significant. They refer to the Acorn Brickworks, Tile Kiln Farm and the various clay pits that, prior to the Twentieth Century, were the dominant industrial feature of this area. Further down the valley, the street name Lime Walk remembers the old associated lime works that also used to be in the Bennetts End area.

The first in an eventual group of eight new shops in 'The Denes' parade at the bottom of Barnacres Road opened in the summer of 1955. This area falls within the Parish of Nash Mills, which is the only part of the New Town to be parished. The Bennetts End Bugle reported that this new sub-centre, which now included shops, a Methodist Church and the rebuilt 'George' public house, "brings much needed amenity to the lower part of the neighbourhood". The main phase of building work at Bennetts End was complete by the end of 1955 and the last significant development for the neighbourhood was the design of a permanent multi-purpose community hall in 1958. The Bennetts End community hall and sports pavilion, situated next to the 'Golden Cockerel', was opened by Henry Brooke MP, the Minister of Housing and Local Government, on 18th April 1959. Built at a cost of £35,000, the construction of this important new facility was a joint venture funded by the Borough Council and Development Corporation. In particular the realisation of a brand new community centre was a triumph for the determined efforts of Bennetts End's own neighbourhood association. For over six years they had operated in temporary wooden huts and had themselves raised, via jumble sales and whist drives etc, a total of over £1,200 towards the cost of the new building. Currently part of the Bennetts End Community Centre is home to a local dental clinic and behind the centre is a modern purpose built doctors' surgery which opened in June 1986.

Long John, one of the principal roads in Bennetts End, features a sweeping terrace of three storey houses, with each alternate house provided with a balcony. The height and curve of this particular housing development is indicative of a Georgian terrace and is a good example of the New Town planners' consistent efforts to introduce a variety of architectural styles into the design of the new neighbourhoods. Although smaller, the neighbourhood centre at Bennetts End is similar in its design to the centre at Adeyfield, with shops in a run of three storey buildings. However the precinct at Bennetts Gate has no concrete canopies over the shops, because instead the maisonettes above project over the pedestrian area. Part of the precinct also features a central grassed area, on sloping ground, which is encircled by the roadway. Directly opposite the neighbourhood centre is the public house which was formerly the 'Golden Cockerel'. Following a tragic murder in its car park in August 1991, it has since been renamed the Greenacres Tavern. Belswains playing fields are close to the shopping centre at Bennetts End; some of this green space adjoins the community centre and forms part of the open ridge of the area. This impressive park, which enjoys spectacular views across the valley, is still known by most of the older residents as 'Coronation Fields'. They were given this name to honour the young Queen Elizabeth who, one year prior to her coronation, toured the local area when the neighbourhood was being built. Further north another important stretch of open ground at Bennetts End is Rant Meadow, which includes an adventure playground and a stretch of woodland close to the St Albert the Great RC JMI School. Together this school site and woodland form a valuable break in what is otherwise a heavily built up area.

Barnacres Road, Bennetts End, November 1953.

Early view of The Denes shopping precinct.

Chaulden

The use of Chaulden as a place name evolved from a corruption of 'Chalkden', a local term which dates back to 1523. This itself comes from the old English 'calc' and 'den' meaning chalk valley. House building started in Chaulden in 1953 and work proceeded sufficiently well for the first houses to be occupied before December. In that first year the Corporation also provided the fledgling community with a temporary meeting place, where religious services and some local social development could begin. Building work on the first four shops for Chaulden also began in 1953. A significant obstacle in the development of Chaulden had been removed when the National Camps Corporation were finally persuaded to dispose of Pixies Hill Camp. Fifteen acres, including the camp buildings, were acquired by the local education authority for school use and the remaining twenty-four acres of the site were sold to the New Town Development Corporation for housing. The old camp buildings at Pixies Hill played an important role in the development of education in the New Town. Pixies Hill served as a 'half way' school, used by children of several neighbourhoods whilst their own new schools were being built. The first children to use Pixies Hill came from Adeyfield in 1953 and most of Chaulden's youngsters went to Pixies Hill School during 1954.

By April 1954 the Boxted trunk water main had been completed and progress on building work was now excellent. By the time of the Development Corporation's annual report in 1955 it was declared that the Chaulden neighbourhood was now half finished. Chaulden Infants School, for children aged between four and seven years old, was completed in January 1955 and a junior school was built on the same site, off School Row. When completed the two buildings were linked by glass walled corridors, so that one kitchen could serve both schools. The Presbyterian Church of England was still using a temporary hut in Long Chaulden for their services, pending the construction of a permanent building and a local Methodist Church, to serve both Chaulden and Warners End, was already being designed. The Chaulden Neighbourhood Council was established early in 1956 and met in a converted hut on the estate provided by the Corporation. In January 1956 the Neighbourhood Council began their own local magazine, called 'The Chaulden Post'.

The following year in 1957 the Chaulden Neighbourhood Centre, offering a total of nine local shops, had been completed. Amongst the first facilities offered were a local launderette, hairdresser, grocer, butcher and Co-op food hall. A local youth club was established in temporary huts at the back of the new shops. A public house called the 'Tudor Rose' was built on Long Chaulden next to the neighbourhood centre and opened later that year.

Chaulden Neighbourhood Centre.

Tudor Rose public house, Chaulden, 1997.

Opening of Chaulden Hall, 15th February 1958. Alderman W. G. S. Crook (standing) with Gilbert Hitchcock (Mayor) and Henry Wells (both left).

Chaulden Community Hall, prior to being re-faced in brick.

Chaulden Primary School.

Playground in Northridge Park.

St Stephen's Church, Chaulden.

United Reformed Church, Chaulden, 1997.

The pub's name celebrates Hemel Hempstead's connection with the Royal Tudor dynasty and in particular the patron of the town's first market charter, King Henry VIII. The new Chaulden Community Hall, built behind the Tudor Rose, was opened on 15th February 1958. This was originally a smaller building of modular design, built in rich Canadian cedar, which has since been extended and refaced in brick. With the opening of this new community centre, the old temporary Chaulden Hall buildings became a full time youth club. There also used to be a small group of shops at the bottom of Long Chaulden in Northridge Way, but these premises now house local doctor and dentist surgeries.

St George's Presbyterian Church was officially opened on Saturday 13th April 1957. This church, situated on the corner of School Row and Long Chaulden, is now a United Reformed Church. St Stephen's C of E Church, opposite the 'Tudor Rose' was dedicated on 12th April 1959 by the Bishop of Bedford. Building work on the Bourne Methodist Church, on a site on the corner of Ashtree Way and Northridge Way, had begun in September 1958. This Church, which opened in April 1959, replaced the existing local Methodist Church in St Johns Road, Boxmoor. By the end of 1959, the main construction work at Chaulden was drawing to a close.

Shops at Northridge Way, Chaulden.

The neighbourhood centre at Chaulden is distinctive, featuring a circular row of nine shops, all in three storey buildings with a projecting canopy and maisonettes above. St Stephen's Church and 'The Tudor Rose' public house were built close enough to be part of these central facilities. Chaulden School backs on the to the local centre and provides an additional communal focus for the neighbourhood. The playing field of the area's other local junior school, Pixies Hill JMI, whose new buildings were erected off Hazeldell Road in 1963, provides a lower buffer between two quite dense areas of housing. Chaulden had to wait another two years for its own secondary school, when the Bourne Valley School opened in September 1965. However this school closed only sixteen years later in July 1981 and its site has since been used for a fresh round of housing development. Chaulden Meadows, on the opposite side of Chaulden Lane, offers extensive playing fields and is home to Hemel Hempstead Camelot Rugby Club. Some of this land is rented from the Boxmoor Trust which acquired its ownership in exchange for land on which Kodak House was built. The meadows were all originally part of the grounds of Chaulden House, of which only the former stable block now remains. Formerly home to the Chaulden youth club, this building has since been renovated and renamed the Isbister Centre. It is now a day centre for people with mental health problems, run by the West Herts Community Health Trust. The large area of open land at Green End, to the east of Chaulden, comprises allotments and school playing fields. The allotment site is the biggest in Hemel Hempstead and this stretch of ground helps to distinguish between the neighbouring communities of Chaulden and Boxmoor. St Rose's RC Infant School is also well wooded on the boundaries of its site which helps to enhance the quality of space between these two built up areas.

At the northern end of Chaulden is the entrance to Shrub Hill Common, where there is an adventure playground which serves both the children of the Chaulden estates and their near neighbours at Warners End. Shrub Hill Common, a surviving relic of old common land which features an ancient green lane in the valley bottom, was officially made a local nature reserve on 10th October 1995. The adventure playground at Shrub Hill is one of three created for the New Town and the establishment of all three was the result of the lobbying and financial support provided by a determined local resident, Mrs. Margaret Lloyd. In 1973 she was deservedly made a Freeman of the Borough, in recognition of her interest and involvement in the provision of facilities for the children and young people of Hemel Hempstead. The use of Shrub Hill is another example of the New Town planners deliberately maintaining a large tract of open land as a shared recreational space, which they also exploited to provide a natural break clearly distinguishing one neighbourhood from another.

High grade houses in Northridge Way, Chaulden.

School Row, Chaulden, prior to additional housing development. The gable of 'Northridge' is just visible on the skyline to the right.

Warners End

The place name Warners End can be traced back to a John Warner who is mentioned in local land documents in 1609. The buildings of Warners End Farm feature prominently on Nineteenth Century maps of the area and occupied a site to the north, later used for Fields End Junior School. A major resource inherited by the New Town neighbourhood was the land which belonged to the estate of Northridge Park, which was a fine family house built by Thomas Micklem in 1890. One of Thomas Micklem's four sons, Nathaniel, enjoyed an outstanding legal career, becoming a Queens Counsel in 1900. He also served as Liberal MP for the Watford Division of Hertfordshire between 1906 and 1910. Nathaniel Micklem retired to the tranquillity of his Northridge estate in 1923, although he always took a keen interest in local affairs. When he eventually died in 1954, aged 100, the house and lands that had been the Micklem family home for 90 years had already been acquired by the Development Corporation to make way for New Town housing at Warners End. Today part of the site of Northridge Park is occupied by a local home for the elderly called William Crook House. This was named after Hemel Hempstead's foremost local historian, Mr. W. G. S. Crook, who was made a Freeman of the Borough in 1965.

Nathaniel Micklem.

Northridge.

Building work on both the estates at Chaulden and Warners End had begun in 1953, although construction at Warners End started later in the year. By the end of 1954 several hundred houses had been built at Warners End and work had begun on the first six shops. A block of garages were quickly adapted to provide a temporary meeting place for the early residents. The hard winter of 1954/5 interfered with some of the scheduled engineering work, but the Development Corporation still managed to complete Warners End Road connecting the new neighbourhood to the town centre.

By the end of 1955 about one third of Warners End had already been completed. However church goers amongst the new residents were still having to travel to nearby Chaulden to worship. Community spirit was nevertheless developing, with several local social organisations already using the temporary meeting hall. Following the dissolution of the early Residents Association, the Warners End Neighbourhood Association was established in December 1957. In this month the first issue of the newly revamped community newsletter, called the 'Warners End Web' first appeared. Warners End's newly built public house 'The Top of the World' opened its doors for the first time at Christmas 1956. The name of this local pub had been chosen to celebrate Sir Edmund Hilary's epic triumph, when he became the first

First shops at Stoneycroft, Warners End.

Western end of Stoneycroft shopping precinct.

Top of the World public house, Warners End.

Stoneycroft Neighbourhood Centre, following refurbishment, 1997.

person to successfully make an ascent of Mt. Everest in 1953. The local Co-op store also opened in December and by 1957 the development of the remaining shops at the Warners End neighbourhood centre had been completed. The St Alban Anglican Church was built at the corner of Long Chaulden and Boxted Road and consecrated by the Bishop of London on Saturday 12th October 1957.

The Warners End neighbourhood was virtually complete in 1959, although temporary buildings were still being used as the local community hall. By 1960 a site for a permanent hall had been reserved in Northridge Way, behind the 'Top of the World'. However local people had to wait until September 1962 when their new community buildings were opened by Sir John Wolfenden CBE. The new community centre offered a large hall with a dance floor, members' club room, lounge bar and kitchen. There was also a clinic wing leased to the County Council, with rooms for a medical officer and health visitors. The construction of the new buildings had been funded by the Borough Council, with contributions from Hertfordshire County Council and the Commission for the New Towns. The converted garages which had been used as a temporary meeting hall for over four years became home to the Warners End Youth Club.

Warners End Youth Club.

Gadebridge House.

Interior of Gadebridge House.

Temporary shops at The Nokes, 1958.

designed as unit workshops and the remaining two units of the block of five were converted into a 40ft x 25ft community hall. This hall at the Nokes was provided by the Development Corporation in order to meet the immediate social needs of the neighbourhood. There was also a small kitchen and a separate Doctors' room which would provide a base for the health visitors. Although completed in the summer, the community hall was officially declared open on Friday, 10th October 1958 by Henry Wells, Chairman of the Development Corporation. The opening of the hall was quickly followed by the establishment of the Neighbourhood Association and a local youth club was formed there in January 1959.

Work had started on fifteen shops at the Rossgate Neighbourhood Centre in February 1958. The centre also included the 'The Gade and Goose' public house which was open by March 1959. Included in the range of shops, opening at Rossgate later in the year, was the butcher, grocer and post office which had transferred from their temporary premises. They had been joined by a chemist, baker, hairdresser, newsagent, greengrocer, dry cleaner and the local housing office.

In the very early days of the Gadebridge neighbourhood, problems were dealt with by a Neighbourhood Committee under the Chairmanship of the

Gadebridge Neighbourhood Centre, 1971.

View of shops and flats at Rossgate.

Baptist Church in Galley Hill, Gadebridge, 1997.

St Peter's Church, Gadebridge.

Gadebridge Community Hall.

Gadebridge Community Centre, following refurbishment, 1997.

Flats at Rossgate, May 1965.

Newly completed houses at Galley Hill, Gadebridge.

Baptist Minister, the Rev. G. Pibworth. As well as street lighting and the lack of a regular bus service, a most urgent problem was the need for local schools. Eleven months after the first residents moved into Gadebridge there were already 100 primary age children living there and work had still not started on the neighbourhood school. Many of the children were transported by coach to the temporary school at Pixies Hill. A first year secondary programme was also provided at Pixies Hill for those children who had reached the age of eleven, but had to wait for Warners End Secondary School to be completed in 1959. Older children attended Adeyfield or Bennetts End secondary schools. Rossgate Primary School was finally constructed off Galley Hill, opposite the neighbourhood centre, in 1959 and opened for the local children in 1960. In the south of the neighbourhood, a second primary school was provided when Gade Valley School opened in 1963.

A secondary school was also built for Gadebridge and this opened in September 1961. The Halsey School, in Fennycroft Road, was named after the Halsey family whose manorial estate, to the north of Gadebridge at Great Gaddesden, dates back to 1544. Nicholas Halsey, who served as High Sheriff of Hertfordshire in 1995, still lives at the old manorial seat which is called the Golden Parsonage. As part of a rationalisation of educational provision by Hertfordshire County Council, the Halsey Secondary School was closed in July 1988 and the remaining pupils transferred to Cavendish School at Warners End.

By 1963 the Borough Council had completed plans for a permanent hall at Gadebridge and in 1964 the Commission for the New Towns, honouring the deal struck with their predecessors the Development Corporation, agreed to contribute over £8,000 towards the total cost of £26,665. The new community centre, situated next to the Gade and Goose, finally opened in September 1965. The Gadebridge Neighbourhood Association had themselves raised £1250 towards the cost of this new facility. Much more recently, the shopping precinct at the Nokes underwent a substantial programme of enhancement. Six years later, on Saturday 1st March 1997, Mayor Mick Young opened an impressively refurbished community centre. The enhanced building now boasts three halls on two floors, with additional day rooms, committee rooms and children's outdoor play area.

The Gadebridge housing estates, which were largely complete by the early 1960's, were to be the most northerly of the New Town's western neighbourhoods. Beyond Piccotts End the more rural environment of Water End and Great Gaddesden is still largely untouched by the Twentieth Century. To the east the Leighton Buzzard Road and Gadebridge Park itself separate the area from the sixth New Town neighbourhood, which was built on the other side of the valley at Highfield.

Crowds gathering in Gadebridge Park on the evening of the Bank Holiday Carnival, August 1968.

St Cuthbert Mayne R.C. Primary School, Gadebridge.

Flats overlooking Gadebridge Park, 1961.

View of the River Gade in Gadebridge Park, 1971.

Highfield

The name of the sixth New Town neighbourhood comes from an old local field name which reflects the obvious geographic feature of the area. Close to the Redbourn Road at Highfield there used to be a sidings and coal depot that belonged to Godwins Halt. This point was the summit of the old Hemel Hempstead to Harpenden 'Nicky Line' branch railway and is an impressive 469 ft. above sea level. This local railway, built in 1877, originally ran in conjunction with the Midland Railway Company and offered a single track passenger service to and from Luton until 1947. Following this the Nicky Line provided a freight only service until British Rail transferred the remaining goods traffic to other lines in 1963.

As early as 1954 the Town Council's proposed layout for the Highfield neighbourhood had been agreed with the Development Corporation, subject to some finer details. By 1959 work had begun on a modern looking neighbourhood, which was to feature housing designs quite different from those used elsewhere in the New Town. Although the housing density was to be quite high, all the properties were to be laid out in an entirely new manner. This new scheme at Highfield intended to offer residents complete freedom from car traffic and also a far greater amount of privacy than would normally have been available on such large housing estates. In 1960, with the exception of some small infilling schemes, all New Town construction work was concentrated on Gadebridge and Highfield. An important and early achievement in the infrastructure for Highfield was the construction of a bridge over the Nicky Line railway, because this new road effectively linked the northern and southern halves of the new neighbourhood together.

By 1961 a total of 123 houses had been completed at Highfield and, as a stop gap measure, a tenants common room had been provided by the Corporation. Work began in October 1960 on a neighbourhood centre and the construction of a local church was also then well advanced. Despite this, the Development Corporation's annual report in 1961 reported serious delays in the progress of house building at Highfield. The report cited bad weather conditions, heavy rain in the summer and autumn followed by an exceptionally hard winter in 1960, as the main factor. These climatic difficulties had been compounded by a temporary shortage of materials and a sudden reduction of staff available in the Corporation's own architect's department.

St Paul's Church of England Church, on the Solway at Highfield, opened in November 1960. It is worth noting that this local church had been built much earlier in the life of its new neighbourhood than most of the churches elsewhere in the New Town. St Paul's was also a church which began with its

Aerial view of Highfield, prior to New Town development, April 1958. Ground has been cleared for the Swallowdale roundabout and the course of Queensway (both left).

Construction work at Highfield, 1969.

The Heights Neighbourhood Centre, Highfield.

The Bellgate Neighbourhood Centre, Highfield.

St Paul's Church, Hemel Hempstead, closed for worship in December 1958.

St Paul's Church, Highfield, 1997.

own sense of history. This new church took its name from the former St Paul's Church, which for 90 years had overlooked Queen Street above Marlowes. As part of town centre redevelopment work this building, which had been erected in 1869, was closed for worship in December 1958 and subsequently demolished. The new Church of St Paul at Highfield cost only £14,000 to construct. The pulpit, some pews, memorial windows and other furniture and fittings from the older church were incorporated into the new structure to seal its link with the past.

During 1962 and 1963 progress on house construction accelerated again, with the Commission for the New Towns building between six and seven hundred new dwellings in each year. Highfield's neighbourhood centre at the Heights opened in August 1962. The facilities it offered to residents were six local shops, two surgeries, an estate office and a small community hall. By 1964 a new public house 'The Royal Stag' had been provided opposite a second neighbourhood centre of ten shops which had opened at Bellgate in Spring 1963. Prior to the arrival of this new shopping precinct, Mr & Mrs Beckett served this part of the neighbourhood from their small post office and general store, located in a private house on the corner of Paston Road and Fletcher Way.

The Royal Stag public house, Highfield, 1997.

Highfield Community Centre, 1997.

The novel ideas that had been used in the planning of the new housing at Highfield were now attracting considerable interest from the architectural profession. As a measure of this success, in 1964 part of the Highfield neighbourhood, which included the shopping centre, was commended in a Housing Ministry competition specifically created to promote good design in housing. By 1965 a local nursery school had been established at the Commission for the New Towns' community centre. This nursery school was run on a non-profit making basis, with the Commission making the property available at a concessionary rate. There were three primary schools eventually built for the children of Highfield. The first was Bellgate junior and infant school which opened in May 1961. The school's name recalls the Bellgate Inn that used to stand at the top of St Marys Road.

Highfield Secondary School opened in September 1963, but only survived for 21 years before being absorbed into the Astley Cooper School at Grove Hill. The Highfield School site which lay between Smithfield and Fletcher Way, was subsequently redeveloped for additional housing from 1985. Hammond Junior School in Cambrian Way, which was built in 1968, was named after local residents Mr & Mrs L J Hammond. This couple were joint authors of books on social history and lived in Dodds Lane, above Piccotts End. The third school, Jupiter Drive JMI, was opened by local MP, Robin Corbett, in

Housing and New Town statuary at Callisto Court, Highfield.

Hidalgo Court, Highfield, December 1976.

September 1975. It was built on open ground opposite 'The Heights' neighbourhood centre.

Jupiter Drive School's unusual name is part of a pattern established on the Highfield estate, which saw several principal residential roads named after planets and features in the solar system. Examples of the street names used are Neptune Drive, Apollo Way, Uranus Road, Pluto Rise, Jupiter Drive, Saturn Way, Mercury Walk and Martian Avenue. The inspiration for this idea reflects the general levels of interest excited by the pioneering Russian and American efforts at space exploration throughout the early 1960's. This sector of housing at Highfield, known as 'The Planets', was the first area to be developed by the Commission for the New Towns. The second sector of the neighbourhood, built further east by the Borough Council, used the theme of 'Hills and Dales' for its street names. A third area around Fletcher Way and Cattsdell still features earlier built council housing, which was provided prior to the New Town development at Highfield.

The main thrust of construction work in the neighbourhood was drawing to a close in 1966. By this time the principal focus of New Town expenditure had switched to the Grove Hill area to the north, and also some redevelopment work around the much older hamlet of Leverstock Green. An important later development in the life of Highfield was the opening of an impressive new community centre at Bellgate on 31st January 1970. This social facility, built at a cost of £40,750, was funded by a partnership involving the Borough Council, the Development Corporation and the County Council, with local people raising money for the internal furnishings. The centre was officially opened by Reginald Freeson, the Parliamentary Secretary to the Minister of Housing and Local Government.

Situated between Church Street and Allandale, Randall Park was the first public park to be provided in Hemel Hempstead. Protected by the New Town planners, it was a gift to the borough by Alderman William Randall, who was Bailiff in 1888 and later served as Mayor and Bailiff of the town in 1902 and 1903. The open land of Howe Grove, adjacent to the A4147 link road with Redbourn Road, defines the northern end of the neighbourhood. The land around Jupiter Drive School, fronting onto Queensway, is another structural break and together with The Heights neighbourhood centre acts as a second community focal point. Included in the facilities available is a modern doctors' surgery which opened on May 9th 1991. Opposite the Heights centre is Highfield House, a listed building owned by Hertfordshire County Council; Queensway old people's home is also close by. Highfield is the only New Town estate to have been provided with two neighbourhood centres. Prior to the construction of Grove Hill, Highfield was also the most northerly of the New Town neighbourhoods.

Grove Hill

Artist's impression of Precinct A, Grove Hill.

Local records identify a William de la Grave in a document which dates back to 1269. However it is more likely that the place name for this, the last neighbourhood to be developed by the Commission for the New Towns, comes from the old English word 'grave' meaning a copse or grove. The name Grove Hill therefore indicates a small area of woodland on a hill. Nineteenth Century maps indicate a large house and estate in the local area, which was then designated using one word as 'Grovehill'. Further evidence of Grove Hill formerly being a well timbered hilltop site comes from the name of a local farmstead 'Two Beeches', which is one of several old farm holdings in the area shown on an earlier map which dates from the Seventeenth Century. The former home of Two Beeches farmhouse eventually became the site for the purpose built community centre which was installed in the heart of the new neighbourhood. The place name 'Two Beeches' is perpetuated locally by sheltered housing for the elderly which opened off Avon Square in 1991. This development replaced an earlier series of sixty-four bed-sits for old people, also called 'Two Beeches', which had been built on the same site in 1971.

A second Master Plan had been produced for Hemel Hempstead in 1960 to show how the population of the New Town could be expanded from 60,000 to 80,000. A key part of this new plan was the development of a brand new neighbourhood, to the north-east of the town, at Grove Hill. By 1964 a draft layout for the first sector of housing at Grove Hill had been produced and in June 1965 the engineering works, necessary to provide the main foul and surface water sewers, had begun. This first area of housing provided by the Commission for the New Towns featured 590 dwellings in a modified Radburn layout. The scheme was similar to that used in the award winning neighbourhood to the south, at Highfield. In response to the tremendous growth in car ownership, for the first time in any New Town neighbourhood a single garage was provided with every house built. The estate also featured over 120 dwellings specifically designed for elderly people and 99 of the houses to be built at Grove Hill were to be for private sale, at prices ranging from £4,600 to £5,175. The scheme at Grove Hill was specifically designed to meet rising expectations and a demand for better quality housing in the New Town. Although the rents were to be dearer, there was to be a higher standard of amenity throughout the development. All the houses were to be provided with warm air gas-fired central heating systems.

Construction work began in October 1966 on what was known as Precinct A at Grove Hill. In a special ceremony on 1st June 1967 Robert Mellish, Joint Parliamentary Secretary to the Ministry, handed over the keys of the first houses to be completed to their respective tenants and purchasers. By early 1969 half the houses scheduled to be built in Precinct A had been finished. Work now began on main access roads to enable other areas of Grove Hill, owned by the Commission, to be developed. The Borough Council planned to provide a further 675 dwellings in one of these areas and plans were also finalised in 1969 for a private developer to build 128 houses in another sector. Another novel feature of the development at Grove Hill was that early provision, at the planning stage, was also being made for areas of land which could be developed by self-build groups and local housing associations.

In 1970 all the 594 dwellings in the Commission for the New Towns' first contract for Precinct A at Grove Hill had been completed. Hertfordshire County Council had opened a local health centre, but other facilities were rather slow to come on stream. In the winter of 1969 a temporary community centre had been created close to the health clinic, by local volunteers moving and redecorating the old builders' site huts used by the original contractors C. Shaw Lovell. When completed the centre, which was owned jointly by the Anglican and Baptist Churches, offered two meeting halls. Nearby, work had only just begun on the first phase of Grove Hill's central shopping development off Aycliffe Drive, where the local supermarket, run by Mr. C. H. Kaye, was open by 1973. It offered a comprehensive food service and included a butchery, chemist, wines and spirits and hardware department. Prior to this Mr. Gray the greengrocer had offered some service to the housewives in Grove Hill by touring the area in his 'big blue van'; one enterprising resident also opened a temporary shop in his house in Aycliffe Drive! The

A view of Henry Wells Square, Grove Hill, 1997.

Greenacres II public house, Grove Hill, 1997.

The Church of the Resurrection and the Community Centre, Grove Hill, July 1977.

Margaret Lloyd Park, Grove Hill, 1997.

The first tenants receive their keys at Precinct A, Grove Hill, 1967.

developing neighbourhood centre had gained a brand new public house when 'The Cupid' opened on 1st April 1971. This pub took its name from the old inn which used to stand on the Redbourn Road and was demolished to make way for a new roundabout at the end of St Agnells Lane. Much more recently this pub has been renamed 'Greenacres II'.

By March 1971 work had begun on the second phase of construction at Grove Hill North. Here the Borough Council had already completed 36 of these new houses, with a further 157 under construction. Roads and services had also been provided for sites at Grove Hill where 99 dwellings were to be built by ten self-build groups, in an area immediately to the west of the council house development. Towards the end of 1973 prolonged negotiations with a major national contractor, for the development of the western sector of Grove Hill, ended in failure to reach agreement. If successful this would have provided a further 1100 houses and flats, available for sale privately. Following the collapse of this plan, and after discussions with the local authorities, it was agreed to make another 40 acres available to the newly established Dacorum District Council. A further 21 acres were reserved for housing associations and self-build groups, with a total of 22 acres at Grove Hill still kept back for private development. In the Spring of 1974 work had begun on a new hall for the temporary community centre at Grove Hill, in order to provide much needed extra space. This was built over a period of a year, with the residents themselves providing the voluntary labour required. In the adjacent neighbourhood centre at Henry Wells Square, several new shops including a launderette, greengrocer, newsagent and chemist, had all opened by the summer of 1975. A large snooker hall called 'Henrys' has since been built behind the main shopping precinct. Meanwhile the Dacorum District Council began work on a further 535 dwellings in the new western sector during that year.

Construction work also started on the long promised community centre in 1975. In common with a pattern already developed, this was to be built jointly by the District Council and the Commission for the New Towns. The Commission had now agreed to contribute the sum of £66,000 towards the total construction cost of £213,000. This impressive new facility was to be an innovation in social planning and ecumenical thinking, offering a large building with a twin function and common entrance. On one side was to be a place of worship, shared by the local Catholic and Anglican Free groups, whilst the other was to be occupied by a large general purpose meeting hall with lounge, kitchen and bar facilities. In December 1976 the first tenants of the western sector of Grove Hill, Mr & Mrs Peter Young of 167 Claymore, were officially handed their keys by Councillor Jack Johnson, Chairman of

Pupils at Grove Hill Secondary School, 1975.

Dacorum District Council and Mr. A. M. Coane, a Director of the building firm, Wimpey. When finished the western sector of Grove Hill would provide a further 535 local authority homes at a projected cost of £5,300,000.

On 16th July 1977 the Church of the Resurrection and Community Centre, which had been built to the rear of Henry Wells Square, was officially opened by the Chairman of Dacorum District Council, Mr. Cyril Fowler. Over 200 people attended the ceremony, including the local MP Mr. Robin Corbett. By this time the twelve year period of building development at Grove Hill was drawing to a successful close. The estate had been deliberately designed to grow at a much slower rate than the earlier New Town neighbourhoods, which had to cope with the peak levels of New Town immigration during the 1950's and early 1960's. Another significant achievement for the community at Grove Hill was the opening of a brand new youth centre in September 1981. This was built just off Stevenage Rise, with many local residents involved in both the fund raising and construction work for this new facility.

An important play area and green space at Grove Hill runs off Washington Avenue, leading out towards Dodds Lane and the open land to the north at Lovetts End. At the southern end of the neighbourhood, below the later western sector, Margaret Lloyd Park is one of the most attractive open areas in the borough. It runs up the slope alongside Piccotts End Lane, which these days is only a footpath, to adjoin the rear of the site for the Aycliffe Drive JMI School which opened in 1974. This local junior school sits on the opposite side of Aycliffe Drive to the neighbourhood centre at Henry Wells Square, which was named after the Chairman of the Hemel Hempstead Development Corporation (1952-1962). In a development similar to that at Highfield, a cluster of local roads in the neighbourhood were named around given themes. In Precinct A at Grove Hill a list of other New Towns, either being built or planned was used. This produced road names such as Basildon Square, Crawley Drive, Stevenage Rise and Livingstone Walk. In Grove Hill North the theme of British rivers was used to provide street names.

The long stretch of Washington Avenue forms the spinal column of the neighbourhood and links into the western sector, where a second junior school, Barncroft JMI, was opened on 11th April 1977. A little further north, at the end of St Agnells Lane, Eastbrook Junior School was built at a total cost of £84,000 in 1973. St Agnells Lane itself defines the eastern edge of the Grove Hill area. Grove Hill Secondary School opened in October 1967, directly opposite the Eastbrook Junior School. In 1986 Grove Hill School, which had been absorbing pupils from the Highfield School following its closure in July 1984, became Astley Cooper School. The large open site of the local secondary school provides a natural break between the Grove Hill neighbourhood and later developments at Cupid Green, which now include the Woodhall Farm estate.

View of Livingstone Walk at Grove Hill, 1969.

Typical example of a Radburn housing layout in Precinct A, Grove Hill.

Woodhall Farm

The successful creation of seven new residential neighbourhoods at Adeyfield, Bennetts End, Chaulden, Warners End, Gadebridge, Highfield and Grove Hill completed the task set for the Hemel Hempstead Development Corporation and the Commission for the New Towns. In addition to redevelopment work in the existing communities of Apsley, Nash Mills, Boxmoor and Leverstock Green, this meant that together they had met the requirements of New Town expansion for Hemel Hempstead, laid down by the Government in the Master Plans of 1947 (amended 1952) and 1960. The subsequent development of a substantial area of new housing at Woodhall Farm has a separate and more chequered history. However it is relevant because this development completes the picture to date, being the eighth distinct new housing suburb to be built around the town centre of Hemel Hempstead. The early days of development work at Woodhall Farm, which involved a partnership between private developers and the Greater London Ccouncil, also offer a revealing contrast to the recorded experiences in the other earlier New Town neighbourhoods.

In 1973 the private development firm of Fairview Estates Ltd. from Enfield were given permission by the Secretary of State to build housing on an initial 34 acre site at Woodhall Farm. It was intended that prices for these new properties would range from £9750 for a flat, to £13,500 for a semi-detached home and £16,750 for a detached four bedroom house. This was to be only the first phase of a much larger development on the entire 169 acre site. The land used had formerly been the main production plant and testing ground for the Brocks Firework Company, who had since moved their operation to Sanquhar, Dumfriesshire, in Scotland. It was Fairview's intention to purchase the land from Brocks in lots, as the scheme progressed over a projected ten year period.

Unfortunately with the combination of roaring price inflation and a depressed housing market that prevailed in the mid 1970's, Fairview Ltd. had chosen a bad time to try to sell their first range of new houses at Woodhall Farm. In order to maintain momentum, the Company tried to sell off large blocks of new housing to the local authority. However Dacorum District Council were unhappy with the specification of some of these early houses and would not agree to purchase them. To everyone's surprise the Company struck a deal instead with the Greater London Council. As a result of this, the first of 250 families from inner London boroughs began to arrive at Woodhall Farm in 1975. Life in the early days was not easy, because it was simply a large housing estate under construction. It was some two miles from the town centre with no shops, schools or social amenities planned. In addition there was no direct bus service and very little in the way of made

Sainsbury's Shopping Centre at Woodhall Farm, 1997.

Doctor's Surgery at Coleridge Close, Woodhall Farm, 1997.

up roads, so that in poorer weather the whole area became a sea of mud. Another problem at Woodhall Farm was the lack of provision made for mains gas and because of this the tenants were forced to run an expensive form of electric warm air central heating. This was doubly galling for the first residents on the new estate, who were also having to pay a higher rent than their Dacorum neighbours, in adjacent areas like Grove Hill. In the first three years that the GLC placed some of their overspill tenants in Woodhall Farm, records reveal that an unexpectedly high number chose to return to the overcrowded Capital. As an example of this, in one street alone, twelve separate families all decided to move back to London.

The Hemel Hempstead Gazette of 7th November 1975, reported that a new beginning was to be made at Woodhall Farm, with the announcement that Dacorum District Council had now decided to sign a £4.1 million development deal with Fairview Estates. In another positive move, the Woodhall Farm Community Association successfully held its inaugural meeting on 5th February 1976. This association eventually secured the use of a converted farm house in Datchet Close as a central meeting place for the neighbourhood. In July 1977 what the Evening Post and Echo was already describing as a "huge new housing estate" began to receive its first direct bus service. This was run by London Country Buses, but was subsidised by Hertfordshire County Council. Many problems were however still unresolved, with a community priest claiming in a local newspaper in February 1978 that many children on the estate were taking tranquillisers because they had nothing else to do! Five years into the life of the new estate there were still no play facilities available for young children and the Eastern Electricity Board was concerned about the number of unpaid fuel bills. Many families simply could not afford to run the expensive electric central heating system that had been installed in their new homes.

A major step forward for the community at Woodhall Farm occurred when Holtsmere End Primary School opened on 26th April 1976. The school was located in Shenley Road, close to the community centre. A purpose built infant block was added at Holtsmere End in September 1981. Brockswood Junior School followed in the Autumn of 1978. The name of this school commemorates the earlier presence of the Brocks Firework Company, whose testing ground formerly occupied the new school site. To mark this connection the Company sent a consignment of fireworks for the school's official opening celebrations on 17th November 1978. In 1979 there were still no shops on the estate and an enterprising shop owner from Gadebridge, Mr. Weston Young, responded by sending a Bedford van to tour Grove Hill and Woodhall Farm two days a week. By April 1980, after years of negotiations, the first houses to be built on the estate were officially handed over to Dacorum District Council. However 115 houses were at first withheld by the

Woodhall Farm Church Centre, 1997.

Community Centre in Datchet Close, Woodhall Farm.

Playtime at Holtsmere End Primary School, Woodhall Farm, 1997.

Flats in Dunster Road, Woodhall Farm, 1997.

GLC from this transfer. Some of these empty houses on the eastern side of the estate then had to be boarded up which angered local residents. The opening of a large Sainsbury's supermarket on 8th December 1981 was a great relief to the local population at Woodhall Farm. This shopping complex, built on a central site adjacent to Brockswood School, also included a chemist, off licence and newsagents. Residents no longer had to travel two miles into town to obtain basic provisions.

Lack of adequate health care facilities however was still a significant problem and in November 1982 Doctors working at Woodhall Farm presented a petition to the local MP, Mr. Nicholas Lyell. At this time the Doctors had already been campaigning for four years and were struggling to cope in accommodation which was a converted two bedroom flat. This served as the only surgery on the estate which by now had a population of 5,000 and was still growing, with an estimated 60 new patients registering each month. Currently the local doctors surgery is in a house on the corner of Coleridge Close, directly opposite the Sainsbury's Supermarket. The long standing problem of energy supplies to the Woodhall Farm estate was finally addressed in February 1983, when Eastern Gas conducted a survey of households to ask who would like gas supplied to their homes.

The Woodhall Farm Church Centre, which is based in a converted house at No. 8 Arkeley Road, was dedicated in October 1986. For over ten years there had already been an Anglican community growing on the estate, inspired by the work of the United Reformed Church minister, Henry Gordon, who moved to Woodhall Farm in 1975. At first services were held in peoples homes, before the size of the congregation dictated that Brockswood School was used as a temporary meeting place. Today the Church Centre is an Anglican Free Church which caters for members of the Church of England, Baptist and United Reformed denominations. In order to help enhance social facilities on the estate, Dacorum District Council decided to fund a bigger and much improved community centre in Datchet Close. Altogether they paid out a total of £340,000 for a brand new hall and additional alterations to the existing building. The association moved into their new accommodation in July 1987 and the keys to the centre were officially handed over by the Mayor of Dacorum, Councillor John Nichols. This proved to be a defining moment in the development of community spirit in Woodhall Farm. The new centre soon flourished and is now home to an impressive range of activities. It plays host to local scout and cub groups, playgroup and nursery sessions, keep fit and dancing classes, lunch clubs for the elderly, indoor bowling and a weekly youth advice service. The Anglican Free Church also holds a regular service in the Centre on the first Sunday morning of every month. After a very uncertain start, the provision of this major social amenity has certainly helped the community of Woodhall Farm to come of age.

Industrial Growth

Sir Patrick Abercrombie's Greater London Plan of 1944, which effectively began the New Town development process in southern England, was itself influenced by the earlier work of the Barlow Committee which had been set up by the Government in 1937. A specific brief of this Committee was to investigate the geographic distribution of the existing industrial population. One principal recommendation produced by the Barlow Committee was the urgent need to disperse industry from already congested urban areas. The idea of 'New Towns' was therefore proposed, whereby industries based in the inner city, together with a working population, could be resettled into new outlying areas.

At Hemel Hempstead, the New Town Development Corporation's first annual report in 1948 indicated that the existing pattern of industry in the local area should be used to help determine the kinds of new employment that would be ideally required in the New Town. A survey conducted in June of that year had revealed that there was 6,200 people currently employed in manufacturing industry at Hemel Hempstead. This represented some 57% of the workforce. No doubt boosted by the large John Dickinson plant at Apsley, 42% of all local employees then worked in the manufacture of stationery, paper, brushes, timber and tailoring industries. A total of 18% of those employed in these trades were women and general wage levels were relatively low. A further 36% of the workforce were employed in service industries and the remaining 7% were accounted for by agriculture, mining and quarrying.

Having identified this pattern, the Development Corporation were now clear that there was an absolute need to encourage more industries which would require a highly skilled workforce, in order to help correct the existing imbalance in local employment. In particular, they wanted to help foster the prosperity of the New Town by attracting more employees from middle income groups. Because the existing demand for female labour was already strong, they also determined that new trades and industries servicing the New Town should predominately require male employees. Taking all this into account, engineering firms operating in London soon became a principal target for the Corporation as the ideal first tenants for the new industrial estate.

The report to the 1947 Master Plan for Hemel Hempstead confirmed that a large site of 219 acres had been identified as the ideal location for an ambitious programme of new industrial development. This area was located close to Cupid Green, in the north-east sector of the proposed New Town. The industrial zone was to be spaciously planned with principal factories

New premises for the Hemel Hempstead Engineering Company, 1950.

Construction site for the Central Tool and Equipment Company, April 1950.

The original Multicore Solders factory being built, October 1951.

Plant for London Ferro Concrete under construction, February 1952.

neatly located on either side of a main avenue. Work began on this area in 1949, with the conversion of the old Ministry of Supply Depot at Cupid Green and the transfer to this site of the Hemel Hempstead Engineering Company. Permanent site preparation work, opening up 106 acres, had begun and the value of the first construction contracts to be let totalled £68,000. By December 1950 a brand new 16,000 sq.ft. factory had been built for the Central Tool and Equipment Company. This company, later known as Centec, came from Richmond and manufactured milling machines for use in the engineering industry. They were the first commercial concern to relocate into the new industrial estate from outside the Hemel Hempstead area. A much larger factory of 92,000 sq.ft. was also under construction for another engineering company, Alford and Alder Ltd., who manufactured front suspensions and axles for the motor industry. Hemel Hempstead was proving attractive to industrialists, of whom over 200 had already made enquiries about possible sites. Firms employing 1,640 people and occupying 261,500 sq.ft. of factory space were now poised to move to the industrial area during the next year.

Progress was rapid and by the end of 1952 four factories had been completed for new employers coming to the town. The 1300 sq.ft. plant for London Ferro Concrete, who made pre-formed concrete sections needed for the construction of other new factory units, had already been extended and the large Alford and Alder factory was now finished. Rolls Razor Ltd, who made electric razors, had moved 200 employees into their newly completed factory and Addressograph Multigraph, manufacturers of office equipment, who employed over 800 people, had moved from Cricklewood into premises which occupied a further 138,000 sq.ft. The largest factory then being planned was to be sited close to the entrance to the new industrial estate on Maylands Avenue and was built for Rotax Ltd. (later Lucas Aerospace). This large plant of 275,000 sq.ft., which cost £1 million to construct, would eventually employ up to 2,000 local people. In January 1952 the Rt. Hon. Harold Macmillan MP, Minister for Housing and Local Government laid the foundation stone for this factory, when he visited to view progress on the industrial estate. By the end of the year over 30 acres of the new area had either been developed or were currently under development. The major concerns who had been installed on the estate had already brought with them over 3,000 jobs.

As far as possible all the new and expanding companies which were moving to Hemel Hempstead tried to bring their current employees with them. One of the most successful in this respect was Alford and Alder who, principally because of the availability of new housing and improved working conditions at their new factory, managed to persuade 92% or their workforce to move with them to Hemel Hempstead. However more commonly, approximately

New factory for the Alford and Alder Engineering Company.

View of Maylands Avenue, showing the Rolls Razor factory.

in 1962 of Hempstead House, situated at the southern end of Marlowes close to the town centre. Approximately half of this impressive development, which provided a total of 120,000 sq.ft. of office space, was to be used to rehouse the computer department of BP Oil Company which was then based in London.

By 1963 the Commission for the New Towns was able to report that there was now little land left on the estate for the introduction of new manufacturing industry. Future development would now have to chiefly concentrate on expanding existing concerns. Over twelve years of continual development by the New Town authorities had created what was then the largest industrial park in western Europe. Total employment on the main industrial estate had now reached 8,854 and the unemployment level in the local area was as low as 1.6% of the total working population. In 1963 a total of 56 companies now had factories on the estate and the planned diversification of industry had continued. In some cases the incoming company built their own factory, in others the Development Corporation built new plant to meet the firm's requirements. Major new concerns such as laboratories of the British Standards Institution and a large distribution centre for J Lyons cake manufacturers were now also firmly established. Fast distribution of goods was becoming increasingly important to modern industries with nation-wide

The first factories built for Atlas Copco and Dexion Ltd. in Maylands Avenue.

Kodak's Colour Processing Plant in Maylands Avenue.

First plant built for DuPont in the industrial area.

Smaller workshop units in Mark Road.

Kodak Distribution Depot in Swallowdale Lane, 1963.

Entrance to the Industrial Estate, Maylands Avenue.

Buncefield Oil Storage and Distribution Depot, which is one of the terminals in the Thames-Mersey pipeline.

ambitions. In 1963 Kodak added to their presence in the town by transferring their entire national storage and distribution system to Swallowdale Lane at the northern end of the industrial estate. This new plant at Swallowdale Lane could now handle the company's total storage of bulk raw materials, as well as their stock pile of factory finished goods for despatch anywhere in the UK.

In 1964 four additional standard sized factories were built in Maxted Road, specifically allocated to companies who could provide suitable employment for school leavers. More than ten years into the life of the New Town, providing sufficient youth employment was now becoming an issue for the Commission for the New Towns. Despite this concern, by the Spring of 1964 unemployment at Hemel Hempstead was registered as only 0.7% of the working population. Back in 1947 there had been 6,200 people employed in manufacturing industry at Hemel Hempstead. Twenty years later this figure had trebled. The 231 acre industrial estate now housed over sixty factories with a combined floor space of three million square feet. By 1968 another major development in the economic life of the town occurred when Kodak Ltd gained permission to erect a large office block on a prominent site close to the town centre. This was to be built near the Plough roundabout and would in future accommodate the Company's National Head Office which was then located at High Holborn in central London. In 1969 a large oil and distribution storage depot was constructed on a 96 acre site at Buncefield Lane. This depot had been built by a consortium of major oil companies and was designed to receive and distribute some 380 million gallons of petrol, kerosene and gas oil annually. The town's first industrial and trade fair, 'Hemex 70', was held at the Pavilion in the town centre from 28th April to 2nd May 1970. Sponsored by the Borough Council this proved to be a great success, highlighting the products and achievements of local firms in Hemel Hempstead.

In September 1971 Kodak opened their new 20 storey head office in Station Road, which would eventually house over 700 employees. Built by Gilbert Ash (Southern) Ltd, a division of the Bovis Group, this tower block was now the tallest in the town. In the course of its construction more than seven hundred miles of steel reinforced rods and over fifty thousand tons of concrete had been used. Its foundations were supported by giant piles driven 40 ft. and 60 ft. into the ground. This new office had been the culmination of eight years of planning and represented a £4.4 million investment in Hemel Hempstead by the Company. As a finishing feature to the new development, Kodak had purchased one of the twelve castings of 'Monument to Balzac' by the great French sculptor Auguste Rodin. It was the only copy to be kept in this country and was mounted on a plinth to stand impressively on the lawned area to the front of the building. In his classic text 'Civilisation', Kenneth Clark described this work of art as the very finest piece of sculpture to have been produced in the Nineteenth Century. This statue was eventually sold by the Company and removed in September 1991. In 1972 Kodak also built a modern training facility in Gadebridge Park. This was a stylish two storey building, which employed a staff of sixty and was known as the Marketing Education Centre.

Another major successful company, who like Kodak had first located to the New Town in 1958, also undertook a major restructuring of their local facilities during the early 1970's. This company, Atlas Copco, formerly from Wembley, was a leading manufacturer of compressed air equipment and rock drilling apparatus. They moved their sales organisation to Swallowdale Lane in 1973, in order to allow the fast expanding manufacturing part of the group to take over their original site. In 1974 the total sales of Atlas Copco amounted to nearly £300 million. Although two heliports had first been rather futuristically included in Jellicoe's original master plan in 1947, the closest the town came to enjoying this facility was following a Public Inquiry in September 1972. Despite objections, particularly from residents of Leverstock Green, Inter City Helicopters Ltd. finally gained planning permission to build a heliport. This was to be situated at a site off Breakspear Way and would be designed to serve the industrial area in particular. However by 1975, mainly because of the changing economic outlook, Inter City Helicopters Ltd. had reluctantly decided not to proceed with negotiations for the lease of the proposed heliport and the scheme died away again. Although plans for a heliport were included in the Dacorum District Plan of 1984, the later development of BP's Head Office on the Breakspear Way site finally put paid to this idea.

In 1977 the fourteen storey office block in the town centre, which housed the computer and accounting centre of BP Oil Ltd., was substantially overhauled. Formerly known as Hempstead House, it was renamed BP House at an official ceremony following an extensive refurbishment programme. It then provided a corporate headquarters for the Company in the town until it was itself succeeded by the major new office development off Breakspear Way. Despite a marked slow down in the growth of manufacturing industry throughout the rest of the country, there were still major new developments in the distribution sector at Hemel Hempstead. In 1977 a new warehouse/distribution centre of 10,800 sq.m. was built by the transport company, BOC Transhield Ltd., to be used principally for the distribution of food products for Marks and Spencer. By 1981 a new release of 4.5 hectares of land for industrial expansion had enabled the Commission for the New Towns to offer a large site to Golden West Foods, who built a bakery and meat distribution centre to serve the highly successful McDonalds nation-wide fast food restaurant chain. In 1983 Kodak Ltd. also enlarged their distribution centre at Swallowdale Lane by building a huge

The Dexion stand at 'Hemex 70' trade fair.

View of Hempstead House.

Head Office of Kodak Ltd, 1971.

Extension to the British Standards Institution's premises, completed 1977.

New Campus Development for 3 Com in Boundary Way, 1997.

Diamond Point, 1997.

Town Centre Development

In their Fourth Annual Report, published in March 1951, the Development Corporation recognised that with such an extensive house building programme well underway, their New Town centre in Marlowes was a key priority. Central facilities would have to be constructed rapidly if they were to cope with the expected growth in population levels. This was to be no easy task because Marlowes was already a functioning trading area, occupied by a haphazard collection of unsuitable buildings. These older properties were a combination of shops, domestic houses and industrial premises that had evolved in an unplanned way over the past 200 years. Although many of the buildings were reaching the end of their useful life and were in a dilapidated condition, some of the older residents were reluctant to leave their homes. The New Town developers were also faced with problems in respect of flooding of the River Gade which ran along the rear of Marlowes, together with old wells hidden in the foundations of some of the older riverside dwellings. To maintain continuity of trading, there was also a need to rehouse some shop keepers and local business people in new accommodation, before demolishing their old premises. Maintaining traffic flows through Marlowes during the construction period was another consideration.

Demolition on the west side of Marlowes, 1954.
The steelwork behind is in preparation for Bank Court.

However the town planners were confident they could overcome all these problems. In July 1952 detailed schemes were agreed for the town centre's main square and central bus station, together with the first group of shopping projects. The first demolition work in Marlowes opened up 515 ft. of shop frontage, but required the demolition of two local places of worship. The congregation of the Bethel Hall planned to build a new chapel in Lawn Lane and the Salvation Army's Citadel was already being rebuilt on a new site provided by the Corporation, adjacent to the new bus station. The first significant new building completed in the town centre was a 26,500 sq.ft. office block, built in 1951 to house the finance department of the major construction firm, Sir Robert McAlpine & Son Ltd.

During 1953 the Town's bus station had been completed for the London Transport Executive and the new market square was beginning to take shape. The Corporation had also built Combe Street and Waterhouse Street, which were the first new roads to be added to the town centre. By the end of the year the first new shops were open in Marlowes and the Development Corporation had submitted to the Ministry an ambitious three year programme for the town centre, which covered the years 1954 to 1956. The intention was that over the next twelve month period, almost the entire west side of Marlowes would be under construction simultaneously. The Corporation would be working, together with private enterprise, to build over one hundred shops in the town centre, with dwellings and office space above. The continuous run of buildings on the west side would be broken at various points, with some shops arranged at right angles in order to provide architectural variety. These shorter pedestrian shopping ways would link into Waterhouse Street to the rear, adjacent to which car parking areas were planned beyond the River Gade and the proposed Water Gardens feature.

By the end of March 1954, the first seven shops in the town centre had been completed and a further 37 were under construction. With efforts concentrated on a large scale redevelopment of the west side of Marlowes, the main street needed to be widened considerably. This was a complex task which involved the realignment of all main services. Towards the end of 1954, Market Square was nearing completion and work was about to begin on Bank Court. Lloyds Bank, Barclays Bank, the National Provincial Bank and Westminster Bank agreed to participate in this unique scheme which involved locating all the banks in the town centre around a new central courtyard, to be created between Marlowes and Waterhouse Street.

By the Spring of 1955, a total of 29 new shops had been completed, mainly around the market square, and a further sixty eight were under construction in Marlowes itself. Combe Street had now been extended over the River

McAlpine office building, built in 1951.

New Town Bus Station.

Hemel Hempstead Market in its new position in Marlowes, prior
to the more recent modernisation in 1991.

Gade and the front of the Water Gardens area, running along Waterhouse
Street, had been grassed over. In July 1955 the town's market was transferred
from its historic site in the High Street, to the new square in Marlowes. By this
time, although far from complete, the shopping centre was already
established as the hub of the New Town.

A year later the number of shops in Marlowes had grown to 49; significantly
Woolworths had become the first major chain store to open in the town
centre, moving from their original site in the High Street. Woolworths soon
had competition from the Co-operative Society whose own impressive
department store, Quality House, was opened by the Rt. Hon. Lord Williams
on 18th August 1956. There had already been a grand opening of a Sheraton
furniture shop, which had been attended by the celebrity comedian and film
star Terry Thomas in June of that year. Another significant retailer arrived
when Sainsbury's new self service store opened in Marlowes on Tuesday,
23rd October 1956.

By early 1957 new premises in Marlowes had also been finished for other
major nation-wide retailers like Timothy Whites, Boots and W. H. Smith.
Professor A. H. Gerrard's design of four panels of sculpted relief on Portland
stone had been erected on the side of one of the larger central store buildings.

Early view of construction work on the west side of Marlowes.

Quality House being built, 1955.

Quality House, completed August 1956.

Restaurant in Quality House.

View of the new town centre from the 'Waggon and Horses'.

*Corner of Bridge Street showing Professor Gerrard's sculpted panels
of the 'Four Stages of Man'.*

View of Bank Court from the Water Gardens.

Newly completed raised shopping area on the east side of Marlowes.

Perhaps inspired by the drawings of William Blake, this work is intended to symbolise the four stages of man's development. It can still be seen on the building at the corner of Marlowes and Bridge Street. The construction of a large roundabout at the southern end of Marlowes had necessitated the demolition of the Plough public house. During 1957 the widening of Marlowes was also completed and there was now a twin carriageway running through two arches of the Nicky Line viaduct, linking into the new Plough roundabout. By the end of the year the construction work on the western side of Marlowes was drawing to a close. The early success of the new shopping centre had however highlighted the need for adequate car parking provision and plans had already been drawn up for a permanent parking area to provide parking space for up to 1150 cars.

The Development Corporation's report, published in the Spring of 1958, triumphantly declared that there was now an almost continuous shopping frontage running along the west side of Marlowes. This run of shops then extended from the Co-op store at the southern end to a point just beyond Market Square in the north. The focus of town centre development work had now switched to the eastern side of Marlowes, where the clearance of old properties was already proceeding rapidly and demolition work was scheduled to be complete by June 1958. The first feature of the development which made up a central shopping area on the east side was to be a block of 14 shops, with a nurses' hostel and 20 maisonettes built above them. This scheme was to be joined by a second larger block of 18 shops, also incorporating 18 flats and 18 maisonettes in a similar three storey structure. There was also to be four larger two storey shops, flanking a courtyard opposite the existing Bank Court, and a six storey office block which would form the third side to this new paved court area.

At the northern end of Marlowes both the Public Library and the Police Station had been completed and were already in use during 1957. At the other end of the town centre, the southern portion of the Hemel Hempstead to Harpenden railway was now being systematically removed and the viaduct across the southern end of Marlowes was demolished in July 1959. This was a major step forward in the redevelopment of the town centre, allowing for an enlargement of the new roundabout which was already struggling to cope with five main road connections. This form of junction was unique in the Country and was provided following extensive research by the Transport and Road Research Laboratory. The new scheme also opened the way for major road improvements to the west which would allow, for the first time, through traffic to by-pass Marlowes and the High Street. By early 1960, eighteen shops on the eastern side of Marlowes had already been let and the first three tiered car park was nearing completion. To decorate the front of this car park, located at the junction of Hillfield Road

Three tier car park at the junction of Hillfield Road, showing the Emett mural.

and Marlowes, a mural was commissioned from the artist and inventor Roland Emett. This ceramic mural is in the form of a cartoon map which depicts features of the local area in the artist's own distinctive style. Although many of the spaces were initially temporary the extensive free car parking facilities, provided by the Development Corporation in and around the new town centre, certainly contributed to the early success of the new shopping area.

The range of new shops and facilities in Marlowes was continuing to draw in shoppers from far and wide and by 1959 there was an increasing interest in securing office space in the town centre. The Ministry of Transport's new office block, on the eastern side of Marlowes, was about to be occupied. Lord Alexander House, a substantial development of 38,000 sq.ft, had also been built behind Marlowes to overlook the proposed water gardens. In 1960 another two large office blocks were already under construction at the southern end of the town centre.

In 1960 the only gap in the new shopping frontage on the west side of Marlowes was occupied by the Luxor cinema. This fine old theatre had avoided demolition, at least until the Rank Organisation could build a new cinema to replace it. Built at a cost of £120,000, and with seats to

View of the old Plough roundabout, 1960.

Nicky line viaduct, immediately prior to demolition.

Lauren Bacall lays the foundation stone for the new Odeon Cinema, January 1959.

The Odeon Cinema, 1960.

accommodate an audience of 1,148, the new Odeon cinema finally opened on Monday 29th August 1960. The foundation stone for this new cinema had been laid by leading Hollywood actress, Miss Lauren Bacall. A grand official opening ceremony was attended by major British movie star Leslie Phillips, who starred in the Odeon's first feature film 'Doctor in Love'. Once the Luxor cinema had been demolished, this only left one commercial building which had survived the changes the New Town had bought to the west side of Marlowes. This was the town's post office, built in the 1930's, whose structure remained unaltered until its frontage was replaced by a modern office premises in 1988.

A survey carried out in December 1960 showed that car parking in the town centre had been increased by 30% from the previous year. However with land values in the town now so high, and spare ground so scarce, the conclusion was that the only way to continue to cope with the increasing success of the town centre was to built more tiered car parks. A second tiered car park was to be provided next to the proposed bowling alley, which was being built behind the shops on the eastern side of Marlowes. In addition to this, a third tiered circular car park was to be part of an ambitious new office accommodation scheme at the southern end of the town centre.

The ornamental water gardens, which run along Waterhouse Street flanking the west side of Marlowes, were completed in 1961. With pedestrian bridges and ornamental flower gardens, they immediately became a very welcome recreation area in the town centre, much appreciated by the general public. The selective floodlighting of the water gardens over the Christmas season was particularly effective. Much increased traffic levels in Hemel Hempstead had given the town planners no option but to enlarge and reconstruct the Plough roundabout in 1961. In an effort to reduce congestion in the town centre, they also added a sixth link for a classified road to run parallel with Marlowes. This new road would eventually by-pass the town centre, joining up with the Leighton Buzzard Road to the north of Piccotts End.

In 1962 several new large stores were constructed on either side of Marlowes, with a pedestrian bridge linking them at first floor level. A similar bridge across Tudor Hill connected with four high level shops constructed further south. During the year the amount of office space provided in the town centre had doubled with the completion of Hempstead House. This unusual office block was a long 'S' shaped four storey building which spanned the southern end of Marlowes on reinforced stilts. This development also included a 14 storey tower block and a four storey circular tiered car park. Altogether it offered a total of 120,000 sq.ft. of office space, of which some 60,000 sq.ft. was to be used to accommodate the computer department of the BP Oil Company, whose headquarters were then still in London.

*The Ambassador Bowling Alley and high level car park
later demolished to make way for the Marlowes Centre.*

View of Marlowes showing the pedestrian footbridge, 1971.

Model of the town centre showing the Hempstead House development.

The spiral car park.

The Ambassador ten-pin bowling alley, with 29 lanes operational, opened in April 1963 and proved to be an immediate success. By the Spring of 1964 a total of 329,500 sq.ft. of office space had been built in the town and a total of 1,275 permanent car parking spaces provided. The County Council had already completed an extension to the library in 1963 and were busy building a principal health centre, with additional accommodation for a divisional office. The construction of an impressive new town hall for the Borough Council, was underway in 1964.

On an adjacent site, work had also begun on a long promised major entertainment venue for the town; this was to be called the Pavilion. Further north, at the far end of Marlowes, the County Council was also financing a range of modern buildings for the Dacorum College of Further Education, which had first been established in 1956. The new campus, which was built adjacent to the River Gade, was completed in 1963 and officially opened in May of that year by the Countess of Albermarle. Three years later the impressive group of buildings which made up the Civic Centre of the New Town had been completed. The Town Hall, Pavilion and Health Centre were all officially opened on 22nd April 1966 by the Rt. Hon. Roy Jenkins MP, who was then Home Secretary.

The twelve year development of Marlowes had inevitably depressed trading activity in the High Street, further to the north. In 1968 a thorough overhaul and redecoration of properties in the High Street was carried out. There was also talk of establishing more specialist trading outlets in this area, in an effort to improve general business levels. Meanwhile in Marlowes two large and impressive new stores, totalling 58,000 sq.ft., were completed in 1970 for Sainsbury's and Boots. Subsequent to this, tenders were accepted from Woolworths for the old Sainsbury's premises and a multiple shoe retailer moved into the former Boots store.

Adjacent to the new Boots premises an additional town centre square had been created on the east side of Marlowes. It featured attractive paving and landscape work, with a flight of steps leading to King Harry Street at the rear. This area eventually became known as Times Square, named after the Times Furnishing Company whose premises were on the south side of the square. This area was further enhanced by the unveiling of a wall mounted sculpture in 1977. Created by British sculptor Richard Browne, this tableau depicts four angelic figures and is called 'Growth'.

Going back to the early days of the Development Corporation, there was always a strong and admirable tradition of displaying public works of art throughout Hemel Hempstead New Town. Not that this has always met with unanimous approval. The magnificent sculpture of the 'Discus

Ministry of Transport office block, also showing the Wimpy Bar at Elizabeth Court.

Ornamental water pool at Elizabeth Court.

Times Square, showing adjoining shops and offices, 1971.

View of Times Square, showing steps to King Harry Street,
before the addition of the 'Growth' sculpture in October 1977.

Bronze 'Monument to Balzac' by Rodin, when it stood in front of Kodak House.

Hamilton House, completed 1974.

Newly built Marks and Spencer store at Selden Hill, 1973.

Thrower', which was originally placed in Bank Court, had a fig leaf added "so as not to offend public dignity". Other modern sculptures, like the 'Reclining Figures' installed at Highfield in 1962, also risked disapproval. Julie Burton, the wife of the local librarian was then quoted as saying: "If it wasn't for the children, I would go to prison to get rid of them". Another Highfield resident also told the local paper that the figures "display something of a sexual nature and were certainly not suitable for a working class town!".

A major new development at the southern end of the town centre was the completion, in September 1971, of a twenty storey office block to serve as a new national head office for Kodak Ltd. This development, which cost £4.4 million to realise, contains 232,000 sq.ft. of office space with adjacent parking for 500 cars. Close to this modern new office block, the town planners had made several attempts over the years to try to tame the ever increasing traffic congestion which plagued the Plough roundabout. Their efforts eventually resulted in a controversial scheme to provide a series of six mini roundabouts around the central area. Introduced in June 1973, this scheme is still with us today and has become known locally as the 'Magic Roundabout'.

One of the last remaining sites in the town centre was finally occupied when Selden Hill was moved in order to accommodate a large Marks and Spencer store. This store, with adjoining shops built by the Commission for the New Towns, opened in June 1973. With a 100 ft. frontage, this new department store offered 31,800 sq.ft. of selling space and provided employment for up to 200 local people. A year later, the development of one of the Commission for the New Towns' last remaining sites in the town centre was complete. This was called Hamilton House and had been built in collaboration with a major pension fund. The development then included five shops with 35,000 sq.ft. of offices above, all of which were immediately let as soon as they were finished.

This project effectively brought to an end the main phase of initial retail development in the new town centre which had taken 21 years to accomplish. The annual report of the Commission for the New Towns, published in March 1976, reveals that the Commission was by then already involved with the local authorities in developing a new Town Centre Policy and Plan. When adopted by the Dacorum District Council, this new document would serve as a basis for further development in the town centre up to 1981. There was already an awareness of the need for new approaches to be developed in order for Marlowes to remain relevant to modern expectations. The main shopping area had become a regional as well as a local town centre, which it was estimated was then serving a catchment population throughout the district of over 150,000.

Aerial view of Marlowes from the south-east, March 1959.

A similar view of Marlowes, sixteen years later in 1975.

Water Gardens

The main scheme to provide ornamental water gardens at Hemel Hempstead was completed in the Summer of 1961. Work had begun one year earlier to canalise the stretch of the River Gade which ran along behind the new Marlowes shopping centre, adjacent to the newly built Waterhouse Street. Large scale earth moving equipment was employed to excavate the area, pushing the soil up to one side, in order to form a new and controlled river course. This work created the required river banks and flower beds, as well as a large artificial mound at the northern end of the feature, close to the Police Station. A concrete base was constructed for the new flow of water, with weirs, waterfalls and fountains incorporated, whilst a host of shrubs and trees were planted along the new river banks.

Lawned areas were laid down to the river from Waterhouse Street and several small pedestrian bridges were then built across the new waterway, linking to the footpaths on the other side which meandered between the new trees and other plantings. In general terms the new water gardens still followed the course of the River Gade. However it was necessary for the scheme to direct the greater part of the river's flow underground, through a large tunnel, to the former gravel pits at Kings Langley, which still act as a holding tank for the Hemel Hempstead area. This arrangement, combined with the construction of a series of weirs, protected the adjacent buildings in the new town centre from the danger of flooding.

Designed by architect and landscape designer Geoffrey Jellicoe, the water gardens were a key decorative feature of his plans for the New Town of Hemel Hempstead. The scheme cleverly creates a sense of space in a restricted area and provides a backdrop which lends some sense of visual unity to the various buildings of the new town centre. The gardens today are home to a wide variety of water fowl and remain a popular attraction for local people and visitors alike. At the northern end of the garden is a children's playground, whilst at the southern end the river opens out into a large ornamental lake. Adjacent to the lake is an area, laid out in the Italian style, which includes seating and an avenue of lime trees. A winding riverside path connects the Italian garden to the children's playground. It also provides access to the public car park areas, which are carefully hidden behind a screen of trees and other plantings.

In the centre of the water gardens lake is an impressive fountain and, nearer Waterhouse Street, an eye catching statue called 'Rock and Roll' by Hubert Yencesse. This sculpture was donated to the town by Henry Wells, Chairman of the Development Corporation, who also arranged for a copy of the statue to go to the new town of Elizabethville in Australia. In return for this gift, the people of Elizabethville sent back to Hemel Hempstead two replica statues by Australian artist John Dowie. They featured two animals native to Australia, the platypus and the kangaroo. These charming models were officially presented to the town on 15th November 1963 by the Agent General of South Australia and were originally sited in a small ornamental pool in the town centre which was re-named Elizabeth Court. Subsequent to the town centre redevelopment work these two pieces have recently been relocated in the Water Gardens.

The Water Gardens scheme received a Civic Trust Award for design in 1965 and is one of the projects by which Sir Geoffrey Jellicoe (1900-96) would like to be remembered. Although his more elegant and grand design for the town centre itself was never realised, the ongoing success of the Water Gardens at Hemel Hempstead is just one fitting tribute to the life and work of this leading landscape designer and architect. Other notable commissions during Jellicoe's long and successful career were the production of a model town centre for the Festival of Britain and numerous garden designs for significant estates like Ditchley Park, Sandringham, Chequers and the Royal Lodge at Windsor. One of his more characteristic creations was the J. F. Kennedy Memorial at Runnymede; he was also responsible for the design of Fitzroy Square in London.

View of the Water Gardens looking north, 1971.

View of Bridge Street from the Water Gardens.

Water Gardens looking north from Bridge Street.

'Rock and Roll' by Hubert Yencesse.

The western side of the Water Gardens, showing footpath and pedestrian bridge across the River Gade, June 1968.

Dacorum College of Further Education

The roots of Hemel Hempstead's principal college can be traced as far back as 1918, when an Efficiency Training Centre was first opened at the John Dickinson paper making factories in Apsley. In addition to offering basic education to young employees for one hour a day in the former works canteen, the Centre also offered evening classes to the general public for a modest fee. When Mr. W. J. Newell took over as Principal in 1923, new technical courses were added to traditional school subjects like English, Geography and Mathematics. Office workers could now learn book-keeping, costing techniques, shorthand and typing etc. After the Second World War the Centre re-opened as the Apsley Day Continuation School. It was now funded by Hertfordshire County Council which appointed five staff, together with the school's first principal, Mr. F. W. Kellaway. However the School was forced to close three years later, when the national school leaving age was raised to fifteen in 1948. Five years later some training activities resumed, when day release classes in engineering began at South Hill School.

The present day college which inherited these traditions was first established in 1956, at the very height of the New Town development work. It was then called the Dacorum Further Education Centre and lessons were originally conducted in a series of old builders huts at Longlands and Field Road in Adeyfield. Mr. A. H. Linton was appointed as the new principal and in 1956 there were already 1,341 day release and evening students enrolled. Within a couple of years the college, with a tutorial staff of over eighty, was offering courses in everything from sheet metalwork to nursing and from electrical installation work to language studies.

With a booming New Town population, rapid expansion in demand for further education quickly outstripped the availability of the college's temporary buildings. Following agreement between the Development Corporation and the various local authorities in 1959, a prime site was allocated for a brand new college campus. This was to be situated at the northern end of Marlowes, adjoining the River Gade. Hertfordshire County Council began building work in 1961 and the new College of Further Education was officially opened in May 1963 by the Countess of Albermarle, although the first new buildings had already been in use the previous winter.

In 1959 Mr. Linton had been succeeded by Mr. Ken McAllister, who remained principal of the college for 18 years until his retirement in 1977. Mr McAllister was succeeded as Principal by Dr G.E.G. Campling in January 1978. The Head of the Department of Adult Studies, Clifford Owen, also retired in 1977. He was the longest serving lecturer at the college, having taught there since the early days of the New Town. During his 31 years in

Hemel Hempstead, Clifford Owen was a leading light in the local community, with a particular interest in fostering the development of the arts and creating a sense of heritage in the New Town. He served as Chairman of the Local History Society and was the first Secretary to the Hemel Hempstead Arts Trust. One of Clifford Owen's particular achievements was his planning of 'International Weeks', under the auspices of which artists and orchestras of international status came to perform in Hemel Hempstead.

By 1981 the college was attracting between 5-7,000 students a year to its leisure class programmes. A total of 1,200 young people were also attending day release classes or full time general education and there were over 500 students enrolled on engineering courses. In April 1991 Dacorum College was merged with Watford College and Cassio College, to become part of the newly created West Herts College. On 1st April 1993 this new foundation was formally incorporated as an independent charitable corporation and continues to expand its activities. The combined college now caters for an impressive total of over 33,000 full and part time students, involved in further, higher and non vocational education. Links with industry have become increasingly important for West Herts College and during the financial year 1995/96 over 1,000 businesses made use of the College's services and tailor made training programmes.

The main entrance to West Herts College, Hemel Hempstead, 1997.

Civic Centre

The site selected for the Civic Centre in the Master Plan for the New Town was on the western side of Marlowes. The proposed new civic area had been deliberately located at the northern end of the main street in an effort to link the various developments in the new shopping centre with the older community in the high street. Building work began in 1962 but the scheme was not finished until 1966. The term Civic Centre was then intended to indicate the suite of newly completed civic buildings which included the Town Hall, the Pavilion and the Health Centre. These three new facilities, all designed by Clifford Culpin & Partners, were officially opened on 22nd April 1966 by the Home Secretary, Rt. Hon. Roy Jenkins MP.

The new town hall featured a single rectangular design with an open courtyard in the middle. On the front of the building there is still a large roundel with a relief of Henry VIII which recalls the significance of the charter granted to the town in 1539. The new building accommodated the Council Chamber and Civic Suite, together with offices for the Town Clerk, Borough Treasurer and Borough Engineer. The Town Hall also housed the borough's public health and housing departments, as well as divisional offices for the County Council's education, welfare, child welfare, civic defence, registrar and probation services. The total cost of the completed town hall building, including furnishings, was recorded as £730,000.

At a speed which was unforeseen by the New Town planners in the early 1960's, the Borough Council unfortunately soon outgrew the accommodation provided by the new building. Today this building is itself referred to as the Civic Centre. Local government reorganisation in April 1974, together with transfer of New Town assets, had considerably increased the District Council's workload and responsibilities. As a consequence many council staff were having to be housed at great expense in rented offices around Hemel Hempstead. In April 1979 a report was presented to the Dacorum District Council outlining the need for an extension to the Civic Centre, in order to bring all employees under one roof and provide a conference room, rest room and extra parking area.

Following the results of a design competition organised by the Borough Council in 1980, the local firm of architects Melvin, Lansley and Mark of Berkhamsted won the contract to design a two storey extension to the Civic Centre. As part of the £2 million scheme, a new island on the River Gade was created, and a 12,000 sq.ft. extension was planned, linking into the existing building via a covered bridge. Construction work of some complexity proceeded during 1981 and staff were finally able to move into the completed offices in the Spring of 1982.

*The official opening of the Civic Centre, 22nd April 1966, showing
Mayor Alistair C. Melhuish with Roy Jenkins (left) and Charles Kirk (right).*

View of the new Town Hall, opened in 1966.

The Pavilion

A central meeting place and social venue was long overdue in the new town centre when work first began on the Pavilion in 1964. The architects Clifford Culpin & Partners produced a specification for an impressively modern building which was completed in the Spring of 1966. The Pavilion, built at a cost of £360,000, was designed as a multi-purpose hall and entertainment venue which could accommodate up to 1,100 people for seated functions. The main hall could cope with up to 500 couples dancing and the small hall, known as the Culpin Room, could hold a further 250 people. The building was suitable for concerts, dances, dinner dances, conventions and exhibitions, but has never been equipped for traditional theatre performances. An ambitious programme of regular events was originally planned. 'Muscles Monday' usually featured professional wrestling or amateur boxing and Tuesday night hosted 'Middle Brow' shows, featuring easy listening music and light entertainment. Wednesday was teenage night, Thursday was given over to classical music and Saturday featured modern ballroom dancing. Friday was left free for private hire. During the day there were lunch time concerts in the Culpin Room called 'Soup, a Sandwich and a String Quartet' and there was a regular Ladies' Afternoon on Wednesdays, featuring a 'Man of the Week' to sing their favourite songs!

Today the Pavilion has become a successful centre of entertainment for the entire district. A full programme of major musical acts, from classical orchestras to chart bands, are hosted along with a variety of stars from many fields of show business. The Pavilion now also has its own public bar and restaurant called 'Snooks'. This opens seven days a week for lunch and hosts a wide range of smaller scale entertainment during the evening.

Massed ranks of dignitaries on the stage for the official opening of the Pavilion, 22nd April 1966.

The Pavilion.

The Magic Roundabout

Ever since it was built in 1957 the Plough roundabout struggled to cope with the ever increasing traffic levels attracted by the booming New Town of Hemel Hempstead. Although enlarged in 1961, this intersection soon became congested again with a continuous stream of traffic from six busy local roads. By the end of the decade, the local authorities were desperate for an answer. In June 1972 the Road Research Laboratory put forward a trial solution. There was some scepticism about the proposed contra-flow mini-roundabout system which would encourage two lanes of two way traffic around the central island. Borough Engineer, Mr. Charles Pratt, described the plan as: "astonishing and somewhat frightening" and many Councillors were far from happy. Instead a more modest scheme of painted spiral markings was introduced to help improve the positioning of vehicles and encourage the possibility of three lanes of traffic moving one way around the roundabout. This idea was given a short trial, but by October 1972 it was announced that the scheme had failed because of "driver behaviour!". There was now no choice but to press ahead and give the more radical proposal a chance. Work began in April 1973 on a scheme which positioned six small roundabouts in a ring around the main island. The scheme came into use on Wednesday 4th June 1973 and the initial confusion was such that all local traffic promptly ground to a halt. At one time, on the first day, traffic on the old A41 road tailed right back into Berkhamsted. However by the following week the arrangement had settled down, as the local drivers became used to the techniques required to navigate the 'magic roundabout' smoothly. The traffic was certainly as busy, but was now moving faster given the continual two way flow. The experiment was deemed a success and what was originally sanctioned by the Borough Council as a six month trial in September 1973 remains with us today.

View of the 'Magic Roundabout', 1980.

The Town Centre Today

Any visitor to Hemel Hempstead in 1997 cannot fail to be impressed by the high levels of new investment Dacorum Borough Council has made to ensure that its principal shopping area remains attractive and relevant to the needs of the community it serves. The indications are everywhere in what is today a bright, confident and modern looking town centre. The roots of this process of renewal, this new and revitalised approach, can be traced back over 20 years to the mid 1970's. A feature article published in the Hemel Hempstead Gazette on 2nd September 1977 proclaimed that the Dacorum Chamber of Trade was worried about the "downfall of Marlowes". The paper reported that most shops and office rents had risen rapidly that year and many local traders were now seriously thinking of moving out of the town centre. The problem was that many of the original leases for shops in Marlowes had first been granted 21 years ago and were now coming up for renewal. The new levels of rent being asked to secure renewal in 1977 were considerably higher; in some cases the proposed charges had risen by 500%! Some of the local shop keepers simply could not afford to continue on this basis whilst others, particularly those occupying the poorer secondary trading locations, were having to consider their future very carefully. Of course once some shops in any town centre are deserted or boarded up, the psychological effect it causes is disproportionately damaging, especially when there is already a struggle to maintain the existing levels of custom.

During the 1970's the downturn in the fortunes of Marlowes had been compounded by increasing levels of competition from other nearby shopping centres. There were good and improving facilities being developed at other major conurbations like Watford, St. Albans, Luton and Welwyn Garden City. In more recent times this level of competition has only intensified, with the spread of huge new shopping malls which attract people from a very wide catchment area. Developments of this kind, first at Brent Cross in 1976 and then Milton Keynes in 1979, began to take increasing levels of business away from Hemel Hempstead. The development of out of town hypermarkets such as Asda at North Watford in 1987 also seriously damaged the prosperity of the town centre. In its heyday, during the late 1950's and early 1960's, the brand new shopping centre at Hemel Hempstead offered very much 'state of the art' facilities. By the time the New Town entered the mid 1970's this was very obviously no longer the case. The Commission for the New Towns acknowledged this position in its annual report of 1979, when it stated that "there is clearly a need to reappraise the town centre to maintain its attraction in competition with other shopping centres". The report also stated that "traffic proposals will be fundamental to any major rearrangement, though it is recognised that the extended layout of the town centre does not easily lend itself to pedestrianisation".

However there were a new range of problems developing in the town centre which were also to have a large influence on the further course of events. In 1978 engineering consultants had been called in to examine certain structural aspects of the bridge over the Tudor Hill. The situation was considered sufficiently serious for the area to be closed to traffic, pending investigations. This bridge, originally intended as a pedestrian link between two storey shops, was little used and it was likely that its removal may be preferable to expensive repairs. In November 1978 a second structure was also beginning to cause concern, when workmen had to remove lumps of loose concrete from Albion Court to protect passers by. A temporary awning was quickly erected to safeguard the pedestrians in King Harry Street. In 1980 an extensive structural examination of town centre properties revealed that a high proportion of the buildings constructed in the 1950's were flawed. Many buildings were suffering from a range of deteriorating problems, caused by the widespread use of high alumina cement. Detailed individual surveys revealed that many of the properties were suffering from structural defects such as defective cladding and spalling concrete foundations. In particular, examination of the large circular tiered car park at the southern end of Marlowes revealed serious problems that it was estimated would cost over £50,000 to repair. On 29th October 1980 the Hemel Hempstead Mail's lead story was "Problems in Town Centre Buildings". By this time the Commission for the New Towns had revealed that between one third and a half of all the buildings in the town centre would require repair work. In addition to this, many of the sounder concrete faced properties that had been built over 30 years ago, now had a very tired and shabby appearance. Commenting on the story Mr Graham Lloyd, then the Commission's Manager in Hemel Hempstead, pointed out that during the 1950's and early 1960's radical new building methods were being tried out, many of which would not be repeated today.

Problems continued to mount and in April 1982 the Government Property Services Agency, which leased the site of Albion House in King Harry Street from the Commission for the New Towns, applied for planning permission to pull down the entire block and rebuild on the site. They had already removed all 160 staff from the premises in October 1981, because they felt that they could no longer guarantee their safety. One year later, in July 1983, things went from bad to worse when large cracks began to appear in the BP building at the southern end of Marlowes. This particular office block was not however affected by the use of high alumina cement; the official reason given at the time for the beginnings of its structural failure was "a combination of ground shrinkage and traffic vibration". Given the imminent danger of collapse, the authorities had no option but to close off the main road which ran beneath the building. The office block was then being leased by BP from the Commission for the New Towns. This problem with what was 'the gateway to Hemel Hempstead" was really the final blow for the 'old Marlowes'. The Hemel Hempstead Mail of 26th August 1983 reported that beleaguered shopkeepers in the town centre were now "nursing their wallets", as the full financial implications of the road closure under BP House started to hit home. In one sense though, it was also a new beginning as the temporary closure of the southern end of Marlowes, caused by the crisis of BP House, had created the ideal opportunity to look again at plans to pedestrianise the town centre. The Eagle Star Property Group purchased the freehold of BP House from the Commission for the New Towns in 1988. Demolition work on the office block began in 1988 and the site was cleared by early 1989.

The process of considering the options for a substantial change to the town centre needed to proceed carefully, fraught as it was with both political and practical difficulties. Not least of which was the fluctuating general economic climate and the continuing uncertainty concerning the structural reliability of many of the principal buildings in Marlowes. In 1987 Dacorum Borough Council finally published a plan in draft form and a public exhibition was held between 7th and 11th July that year. The exhibition illustrated a number of the draft proposals and also created an opportunity for local people to have a say in the shaping of the new town centre. Specific consultations were also carried out with a number of interested parties and a comment form was widely distributed to enable views to be submitted to the Council. The results of the consultation exercise were reported to the full Council in November 1987. They were then incorporated into the final document called the Town Centre Plan, which received its formal approval by the Borough Council on 15th June 1988. In July 1988 David Wass was appointed Town Centres Projects Manager to steer the project through to its conclusion.

The main focus of the Town Centre Plan was straightforward enough. The Council acknowledged that the town was not providing the range of facilities that residents needed; in particular there was now a poor choice of shops. The plan therefore made a commitment to conduct a thorough process of redevelopment that would meet the needs of modern retailers. It was also agreed that there was a lack of comfort in Marlowes; more shops would need to be provided under cover and the overall appearance of the town centre also required considerable improvement. The plan identified that there was still inadequate car parking near the town centre and that a new traffic system was needed to ensure easy access to the car parks provided. The first practical steps in the redevelopment process had taken place in 1987, when a second deck was added to the car parking area adjacent to the water gardens. This increased the parking capacity from 323 to 603 spaces. Both the water gardens and the market were identified in the town centre plan as key assets which needed to be carefully protected in any redevelopment work. The

Borough Council recognised that Hemel Hempstead Market was a colourful and highly popular feature of the town. They were determined to strengthen this particular asset by creating much improved conditions for both stall holders and customers alike. An extensive programme of work was set in motion to achieve just this and the scheme was completed in November 1991.

A key facet of the Town Centre Plan's approach was the proposal to ban all traffic from 'the main shopping core'. This area was defined as being the southern part of Marlowes, between Bridge Street and Moor End Road. Furthermore the plans specified that further north, between Hillfield Road and Bridge Street, the only vehicles allowed in Marlowes would be taxis and buses. The plan also made it clear that for the pedestrianisation scheme to work effectively Wolsey Road and King Harry Street would need to become a one way thoroughfare northbound from Selden Hill to Hillfield Road. As a balance on the western side, it was proposed that Waterhouse Street would need to be one way southbound between Bridge Street and Moor End Road, with a 'bus only' lane operational northbound. The overall effect of these traffic changes was to turn the main streets surrounding the newly pedestrianised town centre into a circular anti-clockwise one way system. The newly pedestrianised area was to be completely overhauled ready to become an attractive new centre for the town. In order to fully realise a high quality scheme for the pedestrianisation works, the Council's architectural advisors, Building Design Partnership, estimated that up to £5 million (1987 prices) would need to be spent on refurbishment. The project involved the complete repaving of Marlowes and Bridge Street, together with landscaping and associated design work. The provision of various ornamental structures, street furniture and some new small shop units was also specified in the plans.

The Town Centre Plan also gave strong support in principle to the provision of a major covered shopping development, which would both enhance and modernise the facilities in the town centre. In the context of the pedestrianisation scheme, the site of any new shopping precinct would need to be at the southern end of Marlowes. By 1987 two rival schemes had already emerged as possibilities. Planning permission was granted by the Borough Council early in 1988 for the first of these, which was a project called the Marlowes Centre. This draft proposal offered a total of 285,000 sq.ft. of new shop floor space, which was to be arranged in three large stores, with a further 53 smaller units all on land to the east of Marlowes. This plan also involved some redevelopment of the existing properties in King Harry Street and Albion Hill. When finished it would provide a large covered shopping centre, at the level of the existing shops, with two mall entrances on the eastern side of Marlowes. The second proposal, a £50 million project, became known as the Lakeside Development.

View of the Water Gardens, showing pedestrian bridges, 1997.

The ornamental lake and fountain in the Water Gardens, 1997.

This project, which centred on the wholesale redevelopment of the site still then occupied by the derelict BP House, was still only at the outline planning permission stage in 1988. Eagle Star, the developers who owned the site, were proposing to produce a scheme which would provide 275,000 sq.ft. of actual floor space on two levels. The detailed plan for Lakeside revealed that the project, like its rival, would produce a large covered shopping area with three large stores, but would only have 36 smaller units.

Construction work began on the Marlowes Centre on 27th June 1988. The excavation work required for the lower levels of the precinct involved massive earthworks, which resulted in over 20,000 lorry loads of material being removed from the site. This was some four years before the beginning of work on the pedestrianisation scheme, of which this new shopping precinct was an integral part. Although the Lakeside scheme was also granted full planning permission, there had always been some doubt as to whether trading levels in the town could sustain two such centres. In this sense the developers of the Marlowes Centre had won the battle between the two rival consortiums by getting their project up and running first. On 4th January 1990 the Hemel Hempstead Herald and Post reported that plans for a second shopping complex had been dropped. Eagle Star were now instead looking at providing a modern office development on the Lakeside site. By this time, the construction of the Marlowes Centre was already drawing to a conclusion. Built at an estimated cost of £32 million, the project had been financed by a three way partnership of developers that included the Church Commissioners For England, Abacus Developments Ltd. (McAlpine) and Imry Merchant Developers PLC. The architect for the scheme was Bernard Engle Architects and Planners. It was planned that the Marlowes Centre would open in September 1990, but work was running about one month behind schedule. However Littlewoods, who had long been one of the scheme's anchor stores, insisted that the September date be adhered to. As a result, for the first month, they were the only shop trading at the Marlowes Centre. At this stage the public had to enter the new precinct through a boarded walkway to screen off all the work still being carried out. The Marlowes Centre was completed in October 1990.

When the project had been completed the developers had successfully created a modern, 'state of the art' shopping precinct, which offered quality shopping in a secure and climatically controlled environment. The Centre originally housed 74 different shop units, although this optimum number has more recently been reduced, when some smaller units were removed to install the current Argos store. The first stores to move into the precinct were Littlewoods, C & A, Dorothy Perkins, Burton, Mark 1 and Spoils. Marks and Spencer were already an integral part of the scheme and a major part of the precinct was built onto the back of their existing store at Selden Hill. As a

Entrance to the Marlowes Centre, 1997.

Interior of the Marlowes Centre, 1997.

Hemel Hempstead Market, June 1997.

Bank Court, June 1997.

principal retail attraction, this gave them considerable extra space virtually free of charge, in order to encourage their continuing investment in the project. Within the original developers' partnership, the Church Commissioners proceeded to buy out both Abacus and Imry to become the sole owner of the scheme. However, as part of a nation-wide restructuring of the Church of England's finances, the Commissioners sold out to a partnership of Bourne End Properties and the Goldman Sachs Whitehall Fund in March 1995. As current owners of the precinct, Bourne End Properties also own the Leighton Buzzard shopping centre and several other similar schemes. Although local newspaper reports revealed in February this year that there was some doubt about the continued involvement of the C & A department store, the latest new stores to recently join the centre have been Virgin and La Senza. As one of the conditions of receiving planning permission in 1987, the Centre had to provide parking for up to 1200 cars. With approximately 62,000 cars per month using its indoor car parking facilities, the shopping precinct currently averages an impressive total of 160,000 visitors a week. The Marlowes Centre has proved to be a very welcome and successful enhancement of shopping facilities in Hemel Hempstead, where it had been carefully designed to blend into the pattern of a redeveloping town centre.

With its major new shopping attraction already secure, work was able to begin on pedestrianisation of the town centre in August 1992. One month previously Borough Councillor Frank Seeley had been quoted in the Hemel Hempstead Herald and Post as saying that the scheme would prove to be "the most significant development in Hemel Hempstead during the last ten years". The local conservation society was fully behind the project; they were glad to see cars being banned from the town centre and also wanted a 'get tough' policy on speeding and car parking laws. By October 1992 the first phase of pedestrianisation, which concentrated on the Bridge Street area, was well under way. Work was proceeding to realign and repave all the roads and pavements in Bridge Street, as well as the northern half of Marlowes as far as the market. A much improved new bus bay was also added during these works. Phase one of the scheme was completed on time, by the end of November 1992. A break was then deliberately planned so that the busy Christmas trade in Marlowes would not be disturbed. Phase 2 began in February 1993 and this was the most intensive period of work on the scheme. It involved repaving the main stretch of Marlowes from Moor End Road up as far as its junction with Bridge Street.

By October, work was also well underway on a revamp of the Bank Court area, with the builders laying a complicated paving design within the courtyard. The design of this paved area came from a suggestion made to Dacorum Borough Council by local resident Sheila Jessop. Her contribution had been part of a public art competition run by the Council in 1992, specifically to encourage the input of local people into the development of the pedestrianisation scheme. The design for the Bank Court paving was inspired by Geoffrey Jellicoe's original plan for the water gardens, which actually had the river running through the centre of the town. Sheila Jessop's design used blue coloured paving stones to trace the path of the River Gade through the Water Gardens feature. Jellicoe had designed the flow of the water in the shape of a snake, with the serpent's head being the ornamental lake and its eye the fountain within.

Phase 3 of the pedestrianisation scheme began in March 1994 and had been delayed a couple of months, because the contractor originally chosen to carry out the work had unfortunately gone into voluntary liquidation. This final phase of the scheme centred on the area of Marlowes between Bridge Street and Hillfield Road. Here work on the realignment and repaving of roads and pavements, including the ramp area, continued until November 1994. When all the work was completed, the total provision of off street parking around the town centre had reached 2,500 spaces. Parking in the water gardens remains free, although charges continue to be made at the Marlowes Centre and the Somerfield and Hillfield Road car parks.

An important aspect of the town centre's improvements was the Shopmobility scheme which the Borough Council first introduced in April 1992. It provides assistance to anyone unable to do their shopping through illness, accident, disablement or age. The scheme offers the free loan of a wheelchair or electric scooter, available from the car park at the Marlowes Centre. In the first phase of pedestrianisation ten disabled parking bays were also established at the southern end of Marlowes, where a 'Dial a Ride' service can be met by a free Shopmobility chair or scooter. Another feature of the town centre improvements was the introduction in April 1994 of CCTV. This closed circuit television system monitors the Market area, Bank Court, Bridge Street, as well as the pedestrianised area. To offer reassurance and security to shoppers and visitors to the town, six cameras in this 24 hour surveillance system are linked to a manned control room. Additional cameras were later installed at the water gardens car park. In time for the completion of the pedestrianisation scheme, the Borough Council also opened an Information Centre in Marlowes. Housed in a brand new circular building, close to the new W. H. Smith store, the centre offers a highly visible central location where visitors and residents alike can ask for advice and information on local matters.

In addition to these specific features, when completed the pedestrianisation project had achieved an entirely new paving scheme for the town centre, together with new seating and litter bins. There had also been extensive

Entrance to the southern end of Marlowes, 1997.

View of the pedestrianised area looking south, 1997.

Children's play area in front of Dacorum Borough Council's
Information Centre in Marlowes, 1997.

'Residents Rainbow', also showing the outdoor cafe in Marlowes, 1997.

View of upper Marlowes beyond Bridge Street, showing 'New Town Growth', 1997.

landscaping work which had involved the planting of many new trees and shrubs. The project had also provided improved street lighting, new bus shelters, various sculptures and pavement designs, an events area and a specially designed toddlers' play space. In the words of Town Centre Manager, Ewan Tilbe, the overall intention was to have created "an attractive, safe leisure area with sculptures, trees and entertainments to give the new town centre a relaxed and Continental feel". When completed the construction cost of the pedestrianisation scheme to the local Borough Council was £2.8 million, of which £125,000 was for commissioned artworks.

At the southern entrance to Marlowes is a large triple arch, constructed in tubular metalwork. This reaches a height of seven metres and frames the main view of the town centre beyond. The green looped design of this arch reflects a similar style of structure to that used in the redesign of the market and all items of newly provided street furniture along Marlowes. Also at the southern end of the town is the 'Residents' Rainbow' by American sculptor Colin Lambert. This was designed to symbolise the aspirations of the first people who moved to the New Town, following the Second World War. In the centre of the town, opposite Bank Court, is perhaps the most attractive example of new artwork in the town. Entitled 'Waterplay' and by leading sculptor Michael Rizzello OBE, it is a wonderful bronze of three children playing in a water fountain. The installation of a water feature at this point is, in part, a historical reference to the ornamental pool that some earlier residents will remember in Marlowes at Elizabeth Court. The sculpture itself also offers some compensation for the removal of the sculpture ' Discobolus' (the discus thrower), which from 1962 used to stand proudly in Bank Court. This impressive bronze cast, which came from a former country mansion at Potten End called Amersfort, has now been repositioned in the water gardens. Another interesting feature in Marlowes is an unusual bronze 3D relief map. This depicts Hemel Hempstead as it was in 1947, prior to the New Town development. It was designed by Graham Thompson and sculpted by John Ravera. The final new feature to be found in Marlowes is a 20 ft. steel tree, which is located close to the Information Centre. This was designed by Peter Parkinson and created by Richard Quinnell OBE and is called 'New Town Growth'. Each panel of the tree represents a different aspect of Hemel Hempstead's past and present. Panels on the tree can be found which, for example, depict the Plough roundabout, the Nicky Line Railway, Brocks Fireworks, Kodak Ltd and the Grand Union Canal. In addition to the distinctive paved design provided at Bank Court, a pavement maze depicting King Henry VIII was laid in the front of Market Square. As a result of the public art competition in 1992, some winning designs have been realised in bronze panels by sculptor John Ravera. As a finishing touch these were set into the paving of the ramp area, once the main pedestrianisation scheme had been completed.

View of Marlowes looking north featuring 'Water Play', 1997.

'Discobolus', relocated in the Water Gardens, 1997.

Jarman Park

The name of Jarman Park comes from the land upon which today's modern leisure development was eventually built. These fields had been owned by the local authority since 1897 when they were purchased by the Hemel Hempstead District Council from Nathaniel Wishart Robinson. In 1954 Jarman Fields were named in memory of Mr. A. H. Jarman, a former Mayor and Freeman of the Borough. Arthur Henry Jarman (1877-1954) was one of a family of seven children born in Hemel Hempstead. First elected to the Borough Council in 1921, he continued in office as Councillor and Alderman until his retirement in 1952. Councillor Jarman worked tirelessly to help develop local health and education services in particular. He occupied the office of Mayor and Bailiff of the town during 1933-35, having the honour of leading the local Silver Jubilee celebrations for King George V and Queen Mary. In recognition of his outstanding contribution Arthur Jarman was made Freeman of the Borough in 1953.

Following completion of Hemel Hempstead New Town in the early 1960's, local debate continued about the best use of the spare ground of Jarman Fields, much of which was then being used as a refuse tip and sewage treatment plant. This debate was no doubt partly fuelled by the fact that a local sports stadium, first proposed in the New Town Plan of 1947, had never been provided. It was in 1966 that the Hemel Hempstead Sports Development Council first suggested that Jarman Fields could be used as a site for a major sports development. Although the need for such a facility was openly acknowledged, the lack of funding then available meant that this proposed initiative could not be carried forward. By 1971 the more commercial prospect of building a £250,000 greyhound stadium on the site, with related facilities for soccer and show jumping, had emerged; but once again this scheme came to nothing.

Despite the lack of progress on the Jarman site, local sporting facilities took a big step forward in 1974, when the Dacorum Sports Centre was built in a joint initiative funded by Dacorum District Council and the Commission for the New Towns. Created around the outdoor Churchill swimming pool, on the corner of Heath Lane and St Johns Road, this new centre offered a brand new indoor 33 metre pool with separate diving pit. The development also included an impressive new sports hall, designed to be used flexibly. This could cope comfortably with most indoor sports, being large enough to accommodate a maximum of ten badminton courts. More recently a gym and high-tech fitness centre was added to the facilities available, offering a range of weight-training equipment and computerised aerobic machines. Currently the Dacorum Sports Centre has embarked on a one year programme of major redevelopment work, which is due to be completed in January 1998.

Further progress seemed likely in 1979 when planning approval was granted for a £3 million scheme, proposed by the Dacorum Athletic Club, to create an athletics arena, ice rink and squash courts on Jarman Fields. However once again lack of financial support meant that the scheme could not be implemented and its planning permission finally lapsed in 1982. Despite all the talk of a large athletics arena, the first development on Jarman Fields had already taken place. This was a much smaller £40,000 project, called the Loco Motion Skate Park. The park was built in 1978 by local businessman Mr. Ron Surrey, who used to run the S & L Ski Shop in Lawn Lane. His company had obtained a seven year lease from the Borough Council on five acres of Jarman Park to build this leisure park for children, which also included a small artificial ski slope. However the craze of skate-boarding during the 1970's proved to be short lived and a new much improved ski slope, together with club room, shop and changing areas, was opened on the site four years later in October 1982. This new ski slope was built on ground formerly occupied by the skate board park, with the original ski-ing facilities retained as a nursery slope.

In 1984 Dacorum Borough Council set about the task of attracting commercial investors prepared to introduce a wider range of leisure facilities on the Jarman Fields site. The Council's outline specification included plans for an ice rink, leisure pool and ten pin bowling, as well as an all weather football pitch, gymnastics centre, indoor shooting range and athletics arena. Eventually in September 1987 Ladbrokes Group Properties Ltd. approached the Council with plans to build a 160 bedroom Hilton Hotel on part of the site. The Company was sufficiently encouraged to return three months later with detailed proposals. These included the development of a large supermarket and major leisure complex, adjacent to their proposed new hotel. By the Autumn of 1988 the Borough Council had formally declared its intention of proceeding to develop these plans, but this decision soon stirred up much local controversy. A considerable body of opinion emerged to claim that sporting facilities should be the clear priority of any new development on the Jarman site. It was further alleged that there was little support in the town for the idea of a new superstore or hotel. A Jarman Action Group was formed and, partly because of local pressure, a Public Inquiry was eventually called by the Secretary for the Environment in September 1990.

A ten day Public Inquiry was held in the Council Chamber of the Civic Centre in February 1991, as a result of which Ladbroke's proposed development finally gained official approval. However by October of that year the scheme had again run into trouble when Rank, partners with Ladbrokes on the leisure side of the development, suspended their interest because of the recession. Ladbrokes then spent much of 1992 trying to seek

Hemel Hempstead's Ski Slope, July 1997.

Tesco Supermarket at Jarman Park, 1997.

out alternative leisure partners for the scheme and, by the end of the year, two new options were offered for the Council's approval. One was from the holding company of Willacre, which traded as David Lloyd Clubs. However this option was rejected because of the view that too many of the proposed facilities would be available to local people, only on expensive 'membership only' terms. The alternative, a revised scheme from Rank, was successful in gaining approval and a binding agreement to proceed was finally signed between Rank and Ladbroke in January 1993. Building began almost immediately in the Spring, with the initial construction work centring on the re-routing of sewage pipes and the laying of gas, water and electricity supplies. Because much of the Jarman site had formerly been used as a refuse tip, the entire terrain had to be compacted with heavy weights to ensure that it was stable enough to build upon. Special measures also had to taken in respect of residual methane which would have accumulated underground in such an area.

In September 1994 a giant Tesco superstore became the first new facility to open on Jarman Park, employing up to 500 full time and part time staff. This building was the first Tesco supermarket to be designed with a glass roof, enhancing levels of natural lighting throughout the store. It was an immediate success and attracted over 40,000 customers during its first week open. The store offers a total of 76,000 sq.ft. of shopping space and also included within the development are a large discount petrol station, parking for 610 cars and a coffee shop. One year later on 25th August 1995, Leisure World was officially opened by the Mayor of Dacorum, Councillor Leslie Taber, and the Chairman of the Rank Organisation, Sir Denys Henderson. The open day was promoted by a Capital Radio Road Show and the level of local interest was so high that the centre had to cope with crowds which amounted to 50,000 visitors over the Bank Holiday weekend. This impressive new entertainment complex immediately became an important addition to the leisure facilities in the town. It offered an eight screen cinema, a restaurant and fast food outlet, two bars, a discotheque and a night club. Sporting facilities built into the centre include a 30 lane ten-pin bowling alley, indoor bowls, snooker and pool tables, an ice rink and an exciting 'Aquasplash' leisure pool. Altogether the £16 million complex covers 250,000 sq.ft., with parking for up to 1000 cars. One month later in September 1995 the Dacorum athletics track was officially opened. This brand new facility was also provided with a changing pavilion and a 200 seater grandstand, although the arena site can cope with a standing crowd of up to 2000 people. The completion of this all weather eight lane running track and athletics field, built to international standards, finally fulfilled the Council's long standing commitment to use some of Jarman Fields to help enhance traditional sporting facilities in the town.

Leisure World, Jarman Park, 1997.

'Aqua Splash' at Leisure World, July 1997.

Dacorum Athletic Track, 1997.

Runners pass the main grandstand, 1996.

Bibliography

CENTRAL OFFICE OF INFORMATION. New Towns of Britain
Pub. 1974 ISBN: 0117006750
COMMISSION FOR THE NEW TOWNS. Annual Reports
Pub. 1963-85
DACORUM BOROUGH COUNCIL. Town Centre Plan
Pub. 1988
DAVIS, E. Hemel Hempstead in Camera
ISBN: 0860233405
DAVIS, E. Hemel Hempstead
Pub. 1995 ISBN: 075240167X
EDWARDS, D.F. Hemel Hempstead in Old Postcards
Pub. 1994 ISBN: 9028857974
Garden Cities and New Towns: Five Lectures
Pub. 1989 ISBN: 0901354509
HANDS, R. & J. Book of Boxmoor
Pub. 1989 ISBN: 0860234193
HASTIE, S. A Hertfordshire Valley
Pub. 1996 ISBN: 0952863103
Hemel Hempstead New Town: The Master Plan Report
Pub. 1947
H. H. DEVELOPMENT CORPORATION. Outline Plan for Hemel Hempstead
Pub. 1949
H.H. DEVELOPMENT CORPORATION. The Development of Hemel Hempstead
Pub. 1952
H.H. DEVELOPMENT CORPORATION. New Master Plan for Hemel Hempstead
Pub. 1960
H.H. DEVELOPMENT CORPORATION. New Town From Old (various editions)
Pub. 1957-61
NEW TOWNS DEVELOPMENT CORPORATION. Annual Reports
Pub. 1948-62
OSBORN, Sir F. & WHITTICK, A. The New Towns: The Answer To Megalopolis
Pub. 1963
OSBORN Sir F & WHITTICK, A. The New Towns: Their Origins and Achievements
Third edition Pub. 1977
ROBINSON, G. Book of Hemel Hempstead and Berkhamsted
Pub. 1975 ISBN: 0860230112
ROYAL ACADEMY GALLERIES. New Towns Exhibition 3-17th October 1959
Exhibition Catalogue Space Pub. 1959
SCHAFFER F. New Town Story
Pub. 1970 ISBN: 0261631705
SHIPMAN, C. & JACKSON, R.. Dacorum Within Living Memory
Pub. 1988 ISBN: 095117737
WALFORD, R. A New Town
Pub. 1968

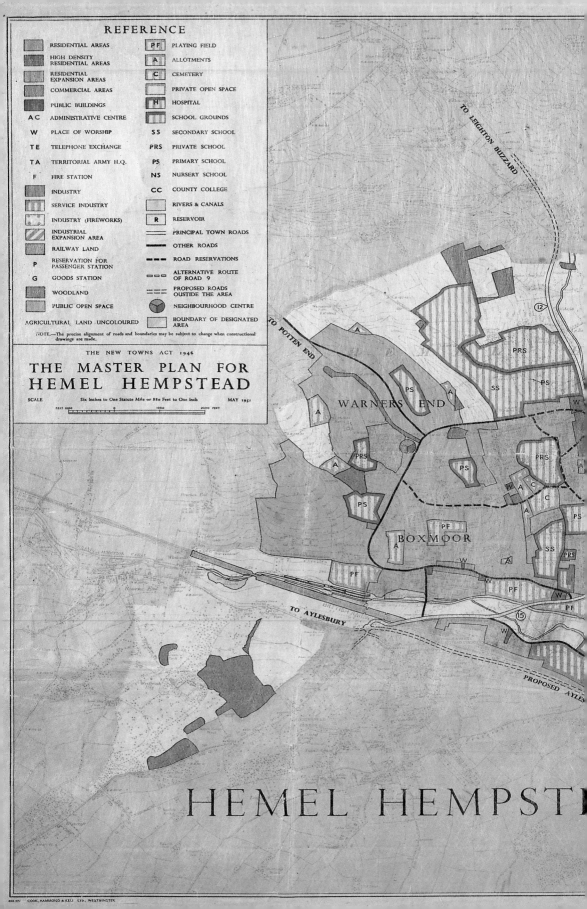

REFERENCE

	RESIDENTIAL AREAS	PF	PLAYING FIELD
	HIGH DENSITY RESIDENTIAL AREAS	A	ALLOTMENTS
	RESIDENTIAL EXPANSION AREAS	C	CEMETERY
	COMMERCIAL AREAS		PRIVATE OPEN SPACE
	PUBLIC BUILDINGS	H	HOSPITAL
A C	ADMINISTRATIVE CENTRE		SCHOOL GROUNDS
W	PLACE OF WORSHIP	SS	SECONDARY SCHOOL
TE	TELEPHONE EXCHANGE	PRS	PRIVATE SCHOOL
TA	TERRITORIAL ARMY H.Q.	PS	PRIMARY SCHOOL
F	FIRE STATION	NS	NURSERY SCHOOL
	INDUSTRY	CC	COUNTY COLLEGE
	SERVICE INDUSTRY		RIVERS & CANALS
	INDUSTRY (FIREWORKS)	R	RESERVOIR
	INDUSTRIAL EXPANSION AREA		PRINCIPAL TOWN ROADS
	RAILWAY LAND		OTHER ROADS
P	RESERVATION FOR PASSENGER STATION		ROAD RESERVATIONS
G	GOODS STATION		ALTERNATIVE ROUTE OF ROAD 9
	WOODLAND		PROPOSED ROADS OUSTIDE THE AREA
	PUBLIC OPEN SPACE		NEIGHBOURHOOD CENTRE
	AGRICULTURAL LAND UNCOLOURED		BOUNDARY OF DESIGNATED AREA

NOTE.—The precise alignment of roads and boundaries may be subject to change when constructional drawings are made.

THE NEW TOWNS ACT 1946

THE MASTER PLAN FOR HEMEL HEMPSTEAD

SCALE   Six Inches to One Statute Mile or 880 Feet to One inch   MAY 1951

FEET 1000   0   1000   2000 FEET

TO LEIGHTON BUZZARD

12

TO POTTEN END

WARNERS END

BOXMOOR

TO AYLESBURY

15

PROPOSED AYLES

HEMEL HEMPST

COOK, HAMMOND & KELL LTD., WESTMINSTER